Foot Regiments

OF THE

Imperial Guard

MICHAEL G. HEAD

with a special section on
Eagles and Colours by P. S. Walton

ALMARK PUBLISHING CO. LTD., LONDON

FRONT COVER: (Left) Caporal of Chasseurs à pied de la Garde, c. 1809. (Centre) Eagle standard, 1804 model. (Right) Lieutenant Porte-aigle, Eagle and Colour of the 1 er Grenadiers à pied de la Garde, 1814.

This book is respectfully dedicated to 'La Sabretache', the Societe des Collectionneurs de Figures, Paris, le plus beau dans le monde. Long may they flourish.

First Published—January 1973

ISBN 85524088 1 (hard cover edition)
ISBN 85524089 X (paper covered edition)

Printed in Great Britain by
Vale Press Ltd., Mitcham, Surrey, CR4 4HR
for the publishers, Almark Publishing Co. Ltd.,
270 Burlington Road, New Malden,
Surrey, KT3 4NL, England

Introduction

THIS volume continues the series of books started with *French Napoleonic Artillery* which will eventually cover all the units of the French Napoleonic army. This book includes the maximum of detailed information for the modeller who wishes to portray the many various styles of dress worn by the foot regiments of the Imperial Guard. Bearing this wealth of detail in mind we feel confident that this work will prove indispensable to the collector and historian alike. At the time of publication no other book in English affords the reader such a comprehensive reference source. The author has consulted many articles and books published in France, as well as contemporary prints and records. In particular the superb prints by Lucien Rousselot, Le Plumet and the magazine of the Sabretache have been most helpful. Thanks are due to Lynn Sangster of Historex Agents for his assistance, to Peter Walton who has provided some material from his files as well as contributing the section covering the Eagles, to Colonel Druene of Paris for supplying copies of contemporary prints from his collection and to many other friends who have assisted in various ways.

The format of the book follows the style established in preceding books, the colour plates being used to show individual articles and the line drawings illustrating the complete uniforms.

Finally the author wishes to express his sincere gratitude for the help of his wife Shirley, in typing and retyping various drafts and manuscripts.

CONTENTS

A night bivouac showing Foot Grenadiers of the Guard. (Private, left, and Drummer, right) standing guard while Chasseurs and their horses rest. Note the piled muskets (left) with the mechanisms well wrapped against damp. A cased regimental standard can also be seen (Colonel Druene Collection).

1: Formation and Organization of the Foot Regiments of the Imperial Guard

IN any book concerned with the Imperial Guard of Napoleon Bonaparte, some attention must be given to the historical line of succession which led to its formation.

Under the Monarchy, the household troops of the King were known as the Maison du Roi. With the advent of the revolution it was only natural that these forces were either disbanded or renamed. In 1791 we find a new organization, raised by the National Assembly, and known as the Garde Constitutionelle du Roi, the King at this time still being the titular head of state. At the same time another organization which owed its allegiance entirely to the new form of government was raised. This was the Garde de l'Assemblée National and was formed from men of the former Gendarmerie Royalle. In 1792 the Garde Constitutionelle was disbanded and the Garde de l'Assemblée was renamed the Garde de la Convention. At this time the Garde consisted of a battalion of infantry and a battery of artillery.

Later known as the Garde du Corps Legislatif, it was merged with yet another organization which had appeared, the Garde du Directoire, to be known as the Garde des Consuls.

It is at this point that the real beginning of the Imperial Guard originated. The Infantry part of the Consular Guard consisted of Grenadiers à pied, Chasseurs à pied and the Marins.

Napoleon signed a decree dated May 18 in the year 1804 which created, from the Consular Guard, his Garde Imperiale. Therefore the senior regiments, later to be known as the Old Guard, were the Grenadiers and Chasseurs.

The regiments of foot will now be briefly described in their order of creation. Appendix 3 summarises and lists all regiments in full.

The Imperial Guard had its own General Staff which consisted in 1806 of four Colonel Generals, namely Marshal Davout for the Corps of Grenadiers, Marshal Soult for the Corps of Chasseurs, Marshal Bessieres for the Cavalry and Marshal Mortier for the Artillery and Marines. There was also an Inspector aux Revues and a Commissioner of War, assisted by 12, later 24 aides-de-camp, a commandant and a captain of engineers. The uniform of this staff is beyond the scope of this book but will be covered in a later work detailing Marshals, Generals and their Aides.

Grenadiers à pied

The Corps of Grenadiers à pied consisted of a HQ staff and at the time of the formation of the Imperial Guard, two battalions of Grenadiers, each made up of eight companies of 102 men, and a battalion of Velites made up of five companies of 191 men.

In 1806 the Corps comprised two regiments, each of eight companies of 122 men and the battalion of Velites (now called a regiment) was the same as in 1804 with the addition of a second battalion of 800 men added in 1805.

In 1808 the two regiments were amalgamated to form one regiment but with the same total strength as a former single regiment. The HQ staff consisted in 1804 of a colonel, a major, three chefs de batallion, three adjutants majors, three sous adjutant majors, two standard bearers, three medical officers, a drum major, three corporal drummers, one bandmaster and 46 musicians. The numbers were modified in 1806 to three majors, each commanding a regiment, six chefs de batallion, six adjutant majors and their sous-adjutant majors, four standard bearers and six corporal drummers. The remainder, ie, the band were unchanged.

A company of 102 men were made up as follows: one capitaine, one lieutenant 'en premier', two lieutenants 'en seconde', one sergeant-major, three sergeants, one 'fourrier' (quartermaster) eight corporals, two sapeurs, two drummers and 80 grenadiers. The foregoing describes in principle the formation of the majority of companies in all the regiments covered in this book but it must be borne in mind that the numbers were sometimes drastically reduced by losses in action, etc, and in many cases a battalion might be reduced to the strength of two or three companies. However, the Old Guard regiments of Grenadiers (and

Grenadiers à pied de la Garde await inspection prior to forming up for a parade.

Chasseurs) were usually brought up to a strength very quickly.

The minimum height for entry into the Grenadiers was 1 metre 80 centimeteres and the entrant had to have ten years military service previously, together with an exemplary record. For this reason the majority of Grenadiers were, to say the least, mature men. The year 1810 saw the addition of the Grenadiers of the Garde Royale Hollandaise to the Imperial Guard. It was at this time that the Kingdom of Holland was dissolved as an entity and incorporated into France, much the same as the 'anschluss' of 1938, where Germany incorporated Austria into the Greater Reich. At first the Grenadiers Hollandais took the regimental number 2 but in 1811, upon the reforming of the second French Regiment, they became the third regiment. The Dutch Grenadiers were disbanded in 1813 after being almost totally destroyed in the Russian Campaign. The first two regiments, however, continued under the restored monarchy as the Corps Royale des Grenadiers de France. One company of the Old Guard Grenadiers accompanied Napoleon into exile and returned with their master during the Cent Jours ('hundred days', a term applied in France to the period starting with Napoleon's return from exile until his final defeat at the battle of Waterloo). During the hundred days the reformed Grenadiers of the Imperial Guard consisted of four regiments, but not alas of the same quality as in former days.

The Chasseurs à pied

The Chasseurs à pied also formed part of the Consular Guard as a company of light infantry. At this time, prior to 1800, the entire company mustered only 94 men.

In 1800 a battalion of Chasseurs was formed consisting of eight companies, each comprising 102 men. The next year saw the formation of a further battalion which raised the strength of the Chasseurs 'en par' with the Grenadiers. Battalions of Velites were raised in 1805. By 1806 the Chasseur Corps consisted of two regiments of Chasseurs and one regiment of Velites. Each regiment comprised of two battalions, each regiment being of eight companies.

Following the example already cited for the Grenadiers, the two regiments of Chasseurs were merged in 1808 and the second regiment reformed in 1811.

During the first restoration the Chasseurs were part of the Royal Guard and took the name Corps Royale des Chasseurs à pied de France. As with the Grenadiers, four regiments of the re-constituted Imperial Guard were Chasseurs during the 100 days.

The composition of the regiments, companies and HQ was identical to the Grenadiers but the band was smaller, consisting of 35 musicians.

Velites

The Velites of both regiments were intended to provide a trained pool from which the ranks of the regiments could be filled.

Formed under the Consular Guard from young men of good families and with good education, they received training to prepare them for entry into the parent regiments. On campaign the two units (ie, Grenadier and Chasseurs Velites) fought as one unit.

A company of Velites consisted of 191 men (170 men in 1806), made up as follows: one capitaine, one lieutenant 'en premier', one lieutenant 'en seconde', one sergeant major, one fourrier, one sergeant, eight corporals, two drummers and 172 Velites. The officers and sous officers (sergeant majors and sergeants) were taken at first from the Old Guard and later corporals of the Old Guard were promoted as sous officers in the Velites.

Companies des Veterans

The veteran companies were composed of soldiers of the Guard who while too old or infirm for active service, could still perform garrison duties, etc.

The force did not exceed the following strength: one Captain, two lieutenants, two sous-lieutenants, one sergeant major, four sergeants, one fourrier, eight corporals, 140 veterans, two drummers.

In 1810 a company of Veterans Hollandais was formed.

The regiments referred to up to this point, with the exception of the Velites and the Dutch Grenadiers, formed the Vielle Garde or Old Guard. The Dutch Grenadiers ranked as Moyenne Garde or Middle Guard.

The Marins de la Garde or Matelots de la Garde

The battalion of Marins was formed on September 17, 1803 and consisted of five 'equipages', each of five 'escouades'.

The establishment of the battalion was as follows: One capitaine de vaisseau as commander of the battalion, one lieutenant de vaisseau as adjutant, five captains de fregate or lieutenant de vaisseau in command of the equipages, 25 lieutenants de vaisseau or enseignes commanding 'escouades', 25 maitres, 25 contremaitres, 25 quarter-maitres, 625 matelots and 5 trompettes. The total strength was 737 men. An equipage consisted of a capitaine de fregate or lieutenant de vaisseau in command, five lieutenants de vaisseau or enseignes commanding escouades, five maitres d'equipages, five contre-maitres, five quartiers-maitres, 125 matelots and one trompette.

Finally the escoude consisted of one lieutenant de vaisseau or enseigns in command, one maitre d'equipage, one contre-maitre, one quartiers-maitre and 25 matelots.

The creation of this unit was a direct result of the plans to invade England by Napoleon when First Consul. They were assigned to the camp at Boulogne where they guarded the invasion boats.

A detachment of 120 Marins formed part of Napoleon's escort at his coronation in December 1804.

In July 1804, the establishment was increased to a headquarters, five equipages and a depot equipage. This made a total of 818 men with a trumpeter or a drummer attached to each equipage. While on service in Spain, the Marins were virtually wiped out and in 1809 consisted of an equipage formed into five escouades. The total strength was 148 men and a trumpeter. Also attached to the Company was a Surgeon-Major and three maitre-ouvriers (Craftsmen).

The Marins were reformed in 1810 into eight equipages and a headquarters giving a total effective strength of 1,136 men and eight trumpeters. It would appear that the losses sustained in combat were not replaced for in 1813 the battalion was reduced to 14 officers and 336 men. When Napoleon abdicated 21 marins and an ensign accompanied the Emperor into exile. They returned with him during the Cent Jours when their strength was increased to 150 officers and men. It should be noted that the ranks of the Marins followed naval form and the equivalents are given in Appendix 1. Also of note is the fact that the Marins had both drummers and trumpeters. The only formation on foot that appears to have had this distinction.

Fusiliers de la Garde

In October 1806 a regiment of Fusiliers, comprising two battalions each consisting of four companies, was formed. The first battalion was formed from the second battalions of the Old Guard Velites. The second from conscripts of the Departmental reserves. The regiment's effectiveness was 1,200 men and it was attached administratively to the Chasseurs à pied. A minimum height requirement for this regiment was five feet two inches which serves to emphasise that the average height in those days was considerably shorter than today's.

In December of the same year, the first battalions of the Grenadiers and Chasseurs Velites were formed into a second regiment and attached to the Grenadiers.

The 1st Regiment became known as the Fusiliers Chasseurs and the 2nd as the Fusiliers Grenadiers.

In 1811 each battalion had a fifth company added which was known as the company of Fusiliers-sergeants. This was probably to provide a reserve of NCO's for the rest of the Guard. These four companies together were referred to as the battalion of Fusiliers-sergeants of the Guard. In December, 1813 a sixth company was added to each battalion. Both regiments were disbanded in 1814 and were not reformed during the Cent Jours.

Tirailleurs Grenadiers

The regiment of Tirailleurs Grenadiers was the first of the new regiments which collectively became known as the Young Guard (Jeune Garde).

Raised by a decree of 1809, the Tirailleur Grenadiers were composed of conscripts. A necessary qualification, however, was the ability to read and write but no doubt this ruling was relaxed in many cases. A second regiment was formed later in 1809 (refer to Appendix 3).

Tirailleur Chasseurs

Two regiments of Tirailleurs Chasseurs were raised at the same time as the Tirailleurs Grenadiers.

Conscrits Grenadiers and Chasseurs

The now almost frantic efforts of Napoleon to build up a large reserve of élite troops begins to take shape as new regiments were added to the Jeune Garde. Unfortunately merely calling them part of the Guard could not endow these young conscripts with the same élan as that displayed by the experienced Old Guard. Therefore, although part of the Guard, the Conscrits Grenadiers and the Conscrits Chasseurs were little better than the standard Line regiment, a fact that must have been recognised as they received the same pay as the Line. (The Old Guard received higher rates and a private of the Old Guard commanded the same respect as a Line sergeant.)

Gardes Nationales de la Garde

This regiment was formed from detachments of the National Guard units of the Northern Departments of France. The National Guard was a form of militia or in more modern terms a cross between the Territorial Army and the Home Guard. The formation of the unit was intended to honour all National Guard units for their work in coastal defence, etc, and was the only unit of the Guard to be organised on Line regiment principles. That is to say a battalion consisted of a company of Grenadiers and a company of Voltigeurs, both classed as Elite or Flank companies as they held the important positions at each end of the regiment lined up in battle order. The remaining four companies of each battalion were Fusiliers, classed as Centre companies. The regiment served mainly with ordinary National Guard units in Flanders and along the Channel coast. This unit became the 7th Regiment of Voltigeurs in February, 1813.

Sapeurs du Genie de la Garde

In 1810, following a serious fire at one of the Imperial residences, Napoleon ordered the formation of a company of Genie whose original function was to maintain and work fire appliances at the various palaces. This company was composed of the following: a capitaine, a lieutenant, a sous-lieutenant, a sergeant major, four sergeants, a fourrier (quarter-master), eight corporals, six ouvriers (consisting of a master tailor, a master rope-maker and four carpenters to maintain the pumps), 32 sapeurs first class, 72 sapeurs second class, ten drivers (conducteurs) and two drummers. The company was equipped with eight pumps and a caisson. The pumps were drawn by two horses and the caisson was identical to that of the artillery arm (see *French Napoleonic Artillery).* The Company was divided into two divisions, each commanded by a lieutenant. Each division was further sub-divided into two sections with two pumps each. The capitaine and two sections were always in attendance at any palace where the Emperor was in residence.

In time of war, the capitaine and three sections were attached to the Imperial headquarters. In 1812, four companies of sapeurs were attached to the infantry of the Guard. Of these four only one company was formed of Guard sapeurs, the other three being Line engineers. The Guard company was attached to the Old Guard division (Grenadiers and Chasseurs), and the Line companies attached to the other three Guard divisions. A second company of Guard sapeurs was formed in 1813.

In 1814 the sapeurs were expanded and organised into a battalion consisting of four companies totalling 615 men. Only the first company ranked as Old Guard and wore the elaborate helmet, the other three wore the shako and ranked as Young Guard. The battalion was dissolved in 1814 and the men were transferred to the 1st Genie Regiment of the Line.

In 1815 a company of Genie de la Garde was formed together with a squad of miners and totalled 125 men. The sapeurs had a minimum height requirement of five feet five inches.

Tirailleurs and Voltigeurs

At one time there were 19 regiments of Tirailleurs and the same number of Voltigeurs. It is suggested that the reader consults Appendix 3 for a detailed list of the dates of formation and disbandment of these regiments.

The first regiments were formed from the Tirailleur Grenadiers (Tirailleurs) and Tirailleur Chasseurs (Voltigeurs). The regiments of Conscrits were also formed into Tirailleur and Voltigeur regiments.

Bataillon d'instruction de Fontainbleu

The original intention of this unit was to furnish trained NCO's for the Young Guard regiments. The high losses amongst officers during the Russian campaign could not, however, be replaced by the graduates of St Cyr (the officers training school) and therefore many of the men at Fontainbleu entered the Guard as sous lieutenants.

Pupilles de la Garde

Louis Bonaparte, while King of Holland, had created two battalions of Velites from the orphans of soldiers and the sons of officers. These were taken into the Guard on the dissolution of the Kingdom of Holland and were known as the Pupilles de la Garde and nicknamed the Garde de Roi de Rome. In the first title the word 'pupille' in this context signifies orphan not student. The second title refers to Napoleon's only son whom he had created King of Rome. Membership was not limited to the orphans of Frenchmen but consisted a large proportion of Italians, Germans and Belgians. The majority of them were aged under eighteen.

Flanqueur Grenadiers

The Flanqueur Grenadiers were formed mainly from the sons of the Gardes Generaux and Garde Forestiers, who were connected with the patrolling and maintenance of Napoleon's Imperial Parks and Forests, and the green of their uniforms was a reminder of their origins.

Flanqueur Chasseurs

Recruited from the same source as the Flanqueur Grenadiers, the Flanqueur Chasseurs were of the same strength. That is, two battalions, each of six companies. Both the Flanqueur regiments had a brief existence of only a year.

2: Basic Uniforms and Equipment

Headgear

IN this volume we are concerned with basically three types of head-dress. First the 'Bonnet à poil' or bearskin, secondly the 'chapeau' or bicorne hat, and lastly the shako.

The bearskin consisted of a leather frame 33 cm in height; with the addition of the bearskin covering the height increased to 35 cm. The Grenadiers' bearskin had a circular cloth patch at the top and a copper plate at the lower front. The Chasseurs, however, had no patch or plate. Both carried a plaited cord, attached at the right upper side and encircling the bearskin. The ends were formed into 'raquettes' or flounders which hung at the right side. At the front top, a tassel, sometimes two in the case of the Chasseurs, was attached on a short cord. At the left side a plume rose from a pom-pon cockade, which was carried approximately halfway up. At the base, hidden in most cases by the ends of the bearskin, was a leather band with a brass buckle which was used to adjust the fit of the head-dress (see Fig 1).

The chapeau worn until 1811 is shown in Fig 2. A later model worn from this time is also shown in Fig 2. Dates are approximate as there would be a considerable changeover period. It will be noted however that the back of the older style was considerably higher than the front. This feature was not as pronounced on the later model, and the 'passants' or stiffeners were revised. At the tips of the chapeau there usually appeared tassels. These were the ends of the cord which was used to adjust the fit. In almost all cases a carrot shaped or round pom-pon was worn and only in rare instances was the large plume carried. At the front the cockade was held in place by a 'ganse' or strap which fastened to a small regimental button.

The shako appears in several forms in this volume and were as shown in Figs 4-7. The first instance we have of the shako was that issued to the Fusiliers Chasseurs and was the 1801 Light infantry model. The construction of all shakos was in the main from black felt, with a leather top and lower band. At the rear a small brass buckle was fitted to the lower band to allow adjustment. In the case of the 1801 model the cockade was worn on the left top side and held in place with a cockade strap fastening to a small regimental button. A pom-pon or plume was carried on the left side above the cockade. The front of the shako was orna-mented with a brass eagle (Fig 4) and the varnished leather peak of black leather was removable and attached by three brass hooks to brass

Fig 1: Bonnet à poil

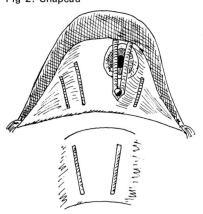

Grenadier
(Side view)

Chasseur
(Front view)

Grenadier
(Rear view)

Fig 2: Chapeau

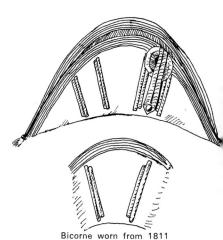

Bicorne worn until 1811

Bicorne worn from 1811

Position of stiffeners at rear of hat are shown
below each item.

Fig 3: Bonnet de Police

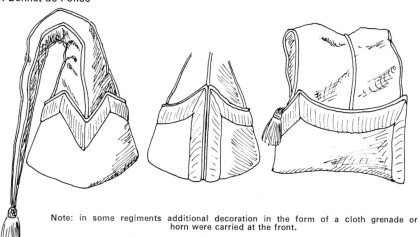

Note: in some regiments additional decoration in the form of a cloth grenade or
horn were carried at the front.

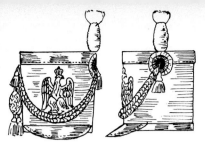

Fig 4: Infanterie Légère shako 1801

Fig 5: 1806 model shako

Fig 6: 1810 model shako

Fig 7: 1810 model in oilskin cover

eyes just above the lower leather band. There does not appear to have been any form of chin strap. This model had virtually disappeared by the end of 1807.

In 1806, the Line infantry, which had up to this point worn the bicorne, were issued with a shako and a similar model was now issued to certain Guard regiments. Following the same method of construction the new model had a pronounced bell shape and also an additional support in the form of 'V' chevrons of leather at each side to stiffen the shako. The cockade and the plume were now carried at the front. The height of the 1806 model shako was approximately 195 mm. Again there appears an almost total absence of chin straps (Fig 5).

A further model was introduced in 1810, being taller and even more bell shaped than the model of 1806. The 'V' chevrons were not used and metal chinstraps were now common, being attached to circular bosses, 'rosaces', just to the rear of the peaks (Fig 6). In both the 1806 and the 1810 models the black varnished leather peak was permanently attached. In some regiments the peaks were edged with a strip of brass or white metal. The height of the 1810 model was approximately 217 mm and the top diameter was 271 mm. It is as well to note at this stage that the shako's worn by the Marins de la Garde differed in many aspects and are covered fully in the section devoted to this regiment.

Mention must also be made of the 'bonnet de police' or field service cap. This is shown in Fig 3, and consisted of a cloth 'fore and aft' cap with a 'V' cut at the front. The centre of the cap rose to a long point which hung over at the right hand side, usually tucked inside the 'fore and aft' section so that the tassel which appeared at the end of the point, protruded over the 'V'. It could also be worn hanging loose. A wide band of lace encircled the cap and came down vertically at the rear seam. The centre portion was piped at the front, rear and on both sides. The various regimental differences are described in Section 3 of this book.

The helmet worn by the Old Guard section of the Sapeurs Genie is described in full in the section dealing with the regiments.

Coats

The first uniform coat was the cut-a-way front, long-tailed habit coat. The collar was 60 to 80 mm high and joined at the front by means of three hooks and eyes. The lapels were of two styles. One with the lower edges square cut and the other with the lower ends pointed. This is shown in Figs 8 and 9. The following applies equally to either type. The lapels were folded back and fastened on each side by six uniform buttons, each 20 mm in diameter, and a further button at the top of each lapel. The top of each lapel was shaped into an 'ecusson' a three pointed shape. The lapels were joined to a point halfway down the chest by means of hooks and eyes. On the right side below the lapel appeared three large uniform buttons. The cuffs matched the shape of the lapels, the lower ends cuffs being pointed also. Where the lapels were square cut the cuffs were straight with a cuff flap. The pointed cuff was approx 110 mm deep from the point and fastened by two 16 mm uniform buttons, one above and one on the cuff. The square cuffs were approx 75 mm deep and the cuff flaps were 110 mm deep by 35 to 40 mm wide. The flap was fastened by three 16 mm buttons. The lower one 20 mm from the bottom of the flap, the second placed centrally and the third 20 mm from the top of the flap.

On each shoulder a 16 mm button was sewn near the collar and a loop of cloth, henceforth referred to as the retaining strap, was used to hold the epaulette in place. Where shoulder straps, as opposed to epaulettes, were worn they were normally sewn in place at the sleeve seam and buttoned to the 16 mm button. In some instances these positions were reversed and the strap was sewn close to the collar and the button sewn near to the sleeve seam.

There were actually five styles of coat tails utilized with the habit coat. Three were long and two were short. From 1801 to 1808 the long tails were folded over to form the turnbacks, as the name implies. From 1808 to 1810, false turnbacks were used. These being sewn into place giving a much tidier appearance. A feature of both these styles was the small triangle of basic coat colour which showed at the bottom. From 1811 the latter style continued but with the absence of the triangle. As can be seen from the drawings (Figs 8-12) the tails grew progressively shorter as time went by. The short tails followed the same styles as the latter two described above. The triangle appearing at first and disappear-

OPPOSITE PAGE: Fig 8: Habit coat (square lapels), 1801-1808. Fig 9: Habit coat (pointed lapels), 1808-1810. Fig 10: Habit coat square lapels), 1811-1815. Fig 11: Habit coat (square lapels-short tails), 1808-1810. Fig 12: Habit coat (pointed lapels-short tails), 1811.

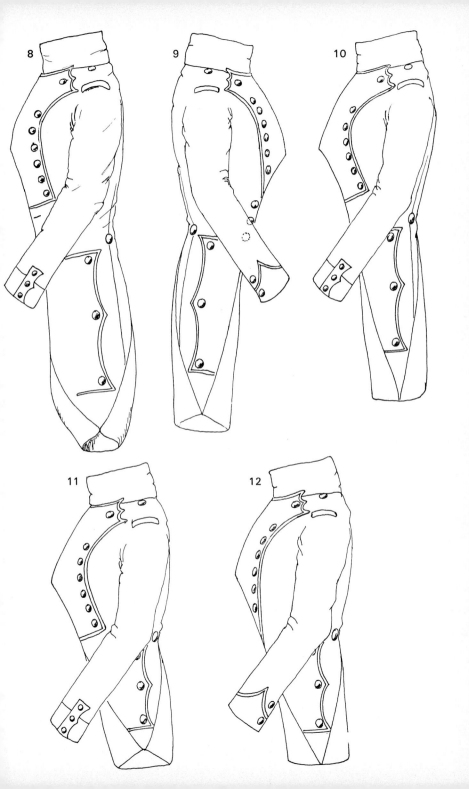

ing in 1811. The pocket flaps were all vertical in the regiments concerned and were three pointed with piping at the edges. The length of the pockets varied with the length of the tails but were approximately 95 mm wide. Three large uniform buttons, 20 mm in diameter, were placed at each point. A further two large buttons appeared on the back seams at the waist.

Another long tailed garment, used mainly for service and petit tenue dress, was the surtout. This style coat fastened down the front with between six and nine large buttons and did not have any form of lapel. The cuffs were either pointed or round (without a cuff flap) and fastened with two buttons. The front of the surtout was cut lower to the waist than the habit coat and obviously the more buttons at the front, the lower the cut was. Most other details were the same as for the habit coats; see Figs 13 and 15.

The regulations of 1812 set out the details for a new coat of a more modern style than the habit coat, which had changed only in detail since the revolution. The new garment, known as the 'habit-veste' or 'spencer', was short tailed with a square cut bottom at the front. The collar, cuff, pocket and shoulder strap details were the same as already described

BELOW: Fig 13: Surtout (seven buttons—pointed cuffs), 1802-1808. Fig 14: Habit veste. Regulation of 1812. Fig 15: Surtout (nine buttons— squared cuffs), 1811.

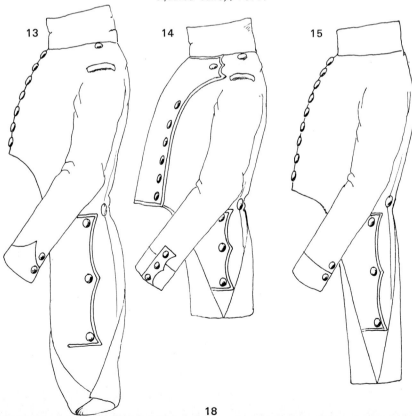

13   14   15

for the habit coat. The lapels which could be crossed over each other or worn buttoned back and hooked down the centre, varied in length depending on the size. They were, however, between 350 mm and 400 mm in depth, 80 mm wide at the waist, about 90 mm wide at the chest and 160 mm across the top. Again the tops of the lapels were ecusson shaped and the same number of buttons were used as on the habit coat. The buttons incidentally were of flat section and stamped to the regimental pattern.

Beneath all these coats a waistcoat was worn with or without sleeves and shoulder straps. The waistcoat or 'veste' buttoned down the front and in most cases had an inverted 'V' cutaway at the waist. Two pocket flaps appeared at each side of the buttons but normally only one was a real pocket, the other just being a flap sewn on to give a balanced appearance.

Legwear

Most regiments wore breeches, buttoning below the knee, and fastening at the waist by two button flaps at the front; see Fig 16. Trousers were also worn, usually on service etc, and were normally white in summer and blue in winter. It is worth noting that in most cases where the word 'white' is used in connection with cloth, this actually refers to the natural undyed yarn which was actually off-white to cream in colour. Some regiments wore, on the march, a cotton 'over-trouser' which was white with light blue lines running vertically. (This cloth was also used for bearskin bags, etc, and was a form of 'ticking' which is similar to the material used to manufacture pillows).

BELOW: Fig 16: Details of Breeches. Fig 17: Two types of gaiters. The long type fastening over, and the short type below the knee.

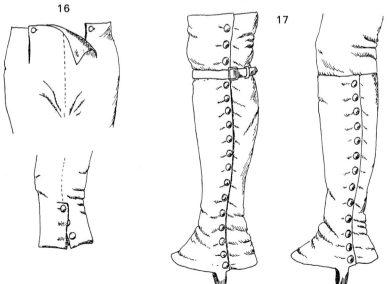

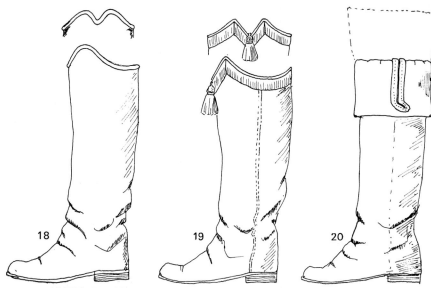

ABOVE: Fig 18: Boot 'à la Souvarov.' Fig 19: Hussar style boot. Fig 20: Kneeboot with top turned over. (Dotted lines indicate position extended).

Gaiters were worn by most regiments, coloured white for summer wear with cloth covered buttons, black for winter wear with brass buttons, or grey for tenue de marche with leather buttons. Most regiments described in this book wore the longer style gaiters coming to above the knee but some wore a shorter version which fastened below the knee; see Fig 17. In tenue de ville or tenue de sortie, white stockings in cotton were worn with buckle shoes. In this case the breeches fastened over the tops of the stockings. Also used extensively in tenue de ville, sortie and other tenues ordinaire were boots 'à la Souvarov'. These were similar to Hussar style boots but the 'V' at the front had rounded tops. No braiding or tassels were worn. Knee length leather boots were worn by officers and musicians, usually with the tops turned down to show a fawn lining and white pulls (Figs 18-20). Overcoats were usually double breasted, with stand up collars, and round cuffs. The coats were buttoned with two rows of between six and eight buttons. At the back a half belt usually appeared with a button at each end.

Equipment

Shoulder belts of cow leather, whitened with chalk, and approximately 70 mm wide were worn over each shoulder in the case of most regiments.

OPPOSITE PAGE: A: Sabre briquet and bayonet belt. (Later style sabre briquet of the Grenadiers à pied). B: Sabre briquet of the Garde de Consuls. C: Method of fastening sabre belt. D: Musket of the Grenadiers à pied; other weapons were very similar. E: Opposite side of lock. F: Detail of butt plate. G: Detail of trigger guard. H: View of pouch showing alternate design of fixing strap. I: Rear view of pouch. J: Underside view of pouch. The two buckles facing the rear attached to the shoulder belt ends. The centre buckle fastened the pouch flap down. K: Front view with flap raised. L: Side view showing field service cap straps. M: End detail of shoulder belt.

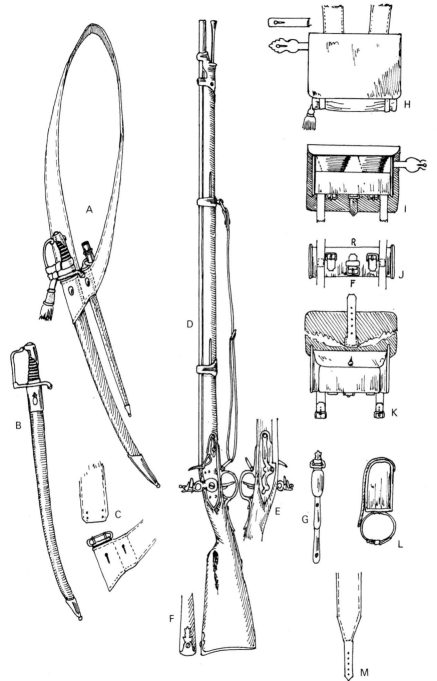

A

B

C

D

E

F

G

H

I

J

R

F

K

L

M

The one passing over the right shoulder was put on first and this belt supported the sabre briquet and the bayonet. The sabre scabbard was of black leather with a brass chape or heel. The hilt of the sabre briquet was brass with filigree leather work and its overall length was 769 mm. The blade was about 595 mm long and the sabre weighed around 1·280 kilos. A sword knot of worsted material was affixed to the hilt as shown in Fig 21A. Also carried on this belt, was the bayonet of steel, between 378 mm and 406 mm long depending upon the date of manufacture; it was carried in a black or brown leather scabbard. The sabre briquet carried from 1804 to 1815 was slightly different in design to that carried under the Consuls; see Fig 21B. The other belt, worn over the left shoulder and passing over the sabre belt, supported a black leather pouch with a varnished flap. The method of attachment of the belt to the pouch is shown in Fig 21H, and this also shows details of the pouch itself.

On the back a cowhide pack was carried on leather straps, the bottom ends of which fastened by means of wooden toggles attached to the bottom of the pack. The pack itself was closed by three leather straps and brass buckles. At the top were two leather loops, through which the straps which held the rolled greatcoat in place passed.

The additional equipment of the drummers and sapeurs is described in detail in Section 4, Têtes du Colonnes, while the officers' equipment is described regiment by regiment in Section 3.

The musket carried by the Old Guard was made especially for their use and all the fittings except the lock were of brass. This musket was 1 metre 44 cm in length. The regiments of the Middle Guard and the Young Guard sometimes carried this musket but it was more usual for them to carry the 'fusil' supplied to the line regiments. In this case the fittings were of iron and the shape of the butt differed slightly from the Guard version; see Fig 21D. In many cases, parts of older muskets were used to repair current weapons, and many were a mixture of parts, both types weighed around nine and a half pounds.

3: Uniforms of the Guard Infantry

IN this section the uniform of each regiment is described, broken down into sections covering head-dress, coats, etc. The figures in the line drawings show the composite figures and in certain instances a full description of a single figure may be given.

Grenadiers à pied   1801-1815

Headgear

The bearskin was of black fur with white cords and flounders. The circular patch at the top was scarlet, as was the plume. From 1801-1802 an aurore cross appeared on the patch. From 1802 until 1808 the cross was white and in 1808 it was replaced by a white grenade. Under the Consuls a yellow brass plate was carried at the front with a rounded top (1801-1804). A design of laurel leaves encompassed the edge with a grenade over a scroll bearing the inscription, 'Garde des Consuls'. In 1804 the design of the plate was changed to the copper design shown in Fig 22A and Plate 1. This featured a crowned eagle with a grenade at each side. The full display of cords and plumes were worn in battle during the early years but in later campaigns only the white tassel at the top front and the pom-pon cockade were worn. When the bearskin was worn with tenue de route the cords and plume were again not worn. The more usual wear on the march was the chapeau, worn with the greatcoat. The bearskin was then carried on top of the pack in a cloth bag made of white cloth ticking with light blue stripes. The plume, when not worn, was carried in a leather cylinder tied to the sabre scabbard.

A drawing by A. Adam in the Musee de l'Armée shows Grenadiers on the march to Moscow wearing oilskin covers over the bearskin. This cover enveloped the bearskin completely and tied at the front.

Sergeants, sergeant-majors and fourriers wore the same bearskin but with the cords, flounders and tassel of mixed gold and scarlet. The grenade or cross depending on the period was also gold.

Officers also wore an identical bearskin but with the cords and flounders, etc, in gold. The plate was in their case gilt.

The chapeaux worn by the men were black with aurore stiffeners and cockade strap. As mentioned in Section 2, there were two styles of chapeau. The tassels which appeared at the ends were scarlet and in the majority of cases a scarlet carrot shaped pom-pon was worn. However, in the early years a cylindrical style of pom-pon with a tuft, again in scarlet, is shown in some contemporary prints.

The Velites wore a chapeau for all occasions, this was black without stiffeners but with the aurore cockade strap and scarlet pull tassels. For normal wear a scarlet carrot shaped pom-pon was worn but for full dress a scarlet plume was used.

NCOs and fourriers had the stiffeners and tassels of mixed scarlet and gold, while the cockade strap was gold.

On the march, or on campaign, when the bearskin was worn, the chapeau was wrapped in the cloth bag already mentioned, and strapped either on top of the rolled greatcoat or at the back of the pack.

The officers' chapeaux had the stiffeners, tassels and cockade strap in gold and in their case the scarlet plume was quite widely used.

In general the chapeau was worn on the march, for tenue de ville and in service dress. After the campaign of 1809, the chapeau was not worn on campaign.

In working dress and similar instances such as tenue d'interieur, the bonnet de police was worn. This was dark blue with aurore lace and piping, NCOs and fourriers probably had gold lace and mixed scarlet and gold piping. Officers had all gold lace and piping. The Velites followed the same pattern.

The wearing of a moustache and the hair tied in a queue was compulsory for the Grenadiers, though many officers did not have the moustache and especially during the latter period of the Empire did not have a queue. The hair was powdered white except when in barracks or on fatigues. Earrings were also worn to such a degree as to state that they too were compulsory.

Coats

At first (1801-2) the Grenadiers had two habit coats, one reserved for full dress and one for service dress. In 1802 the surtout began to replace the second coat. The coat as already indicated was worn for full dress, service dress (until 1802) on some campaigns, and for winter tenue de ville. The three already described in Section 2 were worn and all were of the following colours: Collar plain blue, though in some instances the scarlet linings showed which has given rise to some descriptions quoting scarlet piping. This was never used by the Grenadiers. Squared lapels were the natural unbleached white. The coat was lined scarlet and the turnbacks (in whatever forms) were scarlet. The square cuffs were scarlet with a three pointed white flap.

OPPOSITE PAGE: A: Bearskin plate in copper during the Empire. B: Button of yellow brass. Garde des Consuls. C: Bearskin plate in yellow brass under the Consuls. D: Copper button. Empire Period. E: Pouch under the Empire (eagle and grenades copper). F: Pouch under the Consuls and for the Velites (grenade on yellow brass). G: Gold grenade worn on bearskin patch by officers. H: Officers epaulette. I: Pom-pon Cockade. J: Gorget plate worn by officers when on duty. Eagle and crown were silver. Remainder gilt. K: Officers belt plate. Either all gilt or the eagle and crown silver. H: Officers gold epaulette.

Fig 22

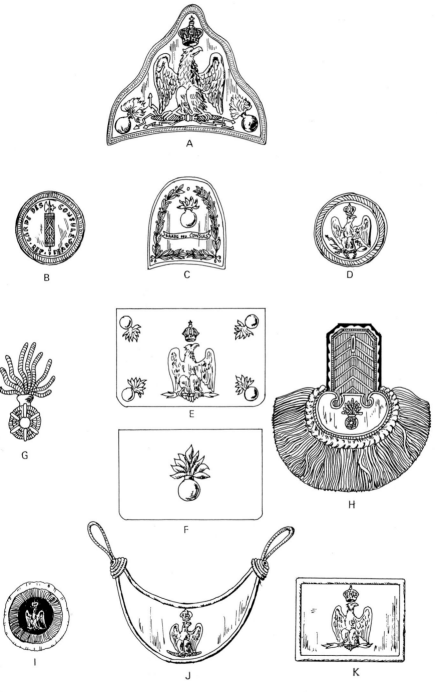

A

B

C

D

G

E

F

H

I

J

K

The vertical three pointed pockets were piped scarlet and the epaulette loops were scarlet lined white. On the turnbacks, aurore woven grenades were worn on a shaped white patch. These grenades were approximately 68 mm in height. Epaulettes were worn on both shoulders and were scarlet, lined white. The Velites wore an almost identical coat but with pointed shoulder straps, blue piped scarlet, in place of the epaulettes. The only other possible difference appears with the cuff flaps. Here it is probable that until 1806 the cuff flaps were three pointed blue piped white. From 1806 the standard Grenadier cuff flap appears to have been used. Under the Consuls yellow brass buttons were worn on the coats but under the Imperial Guard, copper buttons appeared for the men and corporals.

Corporals wore two aurore wool stripes at an angle above each cuff, both stripes being piped scarlet.

Sergeant majors wore epaulettes of gold with mixed scarlet and gold fringes, and gold half moons. The fringes were actually two or three layers, the top or outside one being gold, the one under scarlet. A third outer gold layer was added after 1806 for sergeant majors. Sergeants had gold half moons and scarlet fringes until 1806 and scarlet covered by a layer of gold fringes after. The straps for all NCOs had scarlet lace running the length of the strap, edged by the gold. The underside was lined scarlet. The loops were gold, lined scarlet. On each arm one or two gold lace stripes appeared, piped scarlet. Fourriers or quartermasters wore the aurore stripes of corporals on each arm and in addition an angled stripe of gold lace on each upper arm, the lower point to the front and epaulettes as a sergeant. The turnback grenades for NCOs and fourriers were gold, on a white patch, as were the buttons. With the regiment of Velites, the foregoing applies with the exception of the epaulettes which were not worn. In place of the epaulettes, pointed shoulder straps were worn and were blue piped scarlet.

At the time of their formation the Velites are shown by Bucquoy to have scarlet cuffs and cuff flaps, both piped white but these were soon replaced by the standard cuff as worn by the Grenadiers. Officers wore an identical coat, with gold buttons and grenades, made of a finer material. In their case gold epaulettes were worn according to rank table (Appendix 2) and the illustration in Fig 22H. Around the neck, when on duty, a gilt gorget plate was worn attached by gold cords to the top lapel buttons. The plate was decorated usually by a crowned eagle, or sometimes a grenade in silver, see Fig 22J.

The surtout which was worn in tenue de route in summer, tenue d'interieur, tenue d'exercise, petit tenue and on the campaign of 1806-7 was identical to the foregoing description of the habit coats with the following exceptions. Obviously there were no lapels and the cuffs were plain blue, square cut.

Officers had a surtout, which in some case appears to have piping of scarlet on the front of the coat and lower edges. Some prints show piping to the collar as well. It may well be that in actual fact there was no piping, and as previously mentioned the scarlet lining was showing in both places. With both coats a cravat or neck collar was worn. This was white for parades and black for all other occasions.

Beneath both types of coat a white cloth, sometimes blue, sleeveless waistcoat was worn. In some cases the waistcoat had sleeves but no hard and fast rule as to which was worn can be given. This fastened down the front with 12 small uniform buttons. When doing fatigues (tenue de corvee), this waistcoat could be seen as the main coat was left off. In some cases shoulder straps were attached and in others a white epaulette loop showed on each shoulder.

For some work a smock (sarrau) of white was worn. In appearance this looked like an old fashioned collarless shirt and a figure 'en sarraut' is shown in Fig 25B.

Until 1812, the greatcoat appears to have been plain blue and of the pattern shown here. The greatcoat was worn in tenue de marche or route, and in winter on campaign. By 1812, and possibly before, a scarlet patch with a white edge and a small button appeared on each side of the collar. The cuffs were also piped scarlet. It is unlikely, however, that this pattern was ever in great use and probably a mixture of the two styles could be seen. Rank stripes were worn on greatcoats.

RIGHT: The greatcoat shown in detail. ABOVE: The same garment shown in wear on the Russian campaign in 1812. Note rank stripes on arm.

Legwear

The following trousers or breeches were worn and by referring to the list of 'tenues' following the section on equipment, the reader may ascertain in which circumstances and with what other apparel any particular garment appeared.

The knee length breeches were either white or blue, and buttoned with two cloth covered buttons below the knee and to the outside. Between 1805 and 1808, fawn breeches appear to have been worn with white stockings in tenue de ville. Also during an inspection in 1806 trousers of blue, white and of light blue and white cotton were worn on campaign and tenue de route. Gaiters coming to above the knee were worn. White for parade and summer wear, black for winter and campaign. Between 1803-4, grey gaiters were used for tenue de marche. The white gaiters were buttoned by white cloth covered buttons, 18 in all while the black and grey gaiters had brass buttons. A strap and buckle fastened them just below the knee. Boots were black leather.

In tenue de sortie during the winter black leather boots, 'à la Souvarov' were worn. They are shown in Fig 18. Officers wore black leather knee boots, turned down to show the fawn lining and white pull straps, on most occasions. White gaiters however, were worn on full dress parades. White cotton, or silk in some cases for officers, stockings were worn with the breeches fastening over the top in tenue de ville and tenue de societé.

Black shoes with metal buckles were worn with the stockings for tenue de ville.

Equipment

The men carried the two shoulder belts supporting the sabre briquet, bayonet and pouch. The sword knot on the hilt of the sabre briquet was white with a scarlet knot and tassel. NCOs and fourriers had a sword knot of mixed gold and scarlet. For tenue de ville the NCOs carried an epée supported by a waist belt under the front flap, in place of the sabre briquet. The pouch was not carried by any rank in tenue de ville. The edges of the belts were stitched. The flap of the pouch carried in the centre an embossed copper eagle and a copper grenade in each corner with the flame of the grenade pointing to the centre; see Fig 22E The bonnet de police was rolled and strapped under the pouch (see Fig 21H for detail).

On campaign a cloth cover was placed over the pouch flap from around 1805. This was white with the eagle and grenades painted on in black. Another example is in black cloth with yellow painted eagle and grenades. The cowskin pack was carried in full dress and on campaign (see Section 2).

The fusil had a whitened leather sling attached. The fusil was carried at the trail, with the forefinger through the trigger guard, at the righthand side by NCOs and held to the left shoulder by the left arm pressing across the chest by the men. Officers carried a light sword or epée with a straight blade. This was usually supported, in a black leather scabbard, heeled with gilt, by a waist belt.

Almost invariably the waist belt passed over the waistcoat, but could be worn under the trouser flap. An oblong plate of gilt with either an eagle or a grenade embossed on it, was worn on the belt. The belt was normally white but some examples are shown in black. In the 1st Regiment, the colonel-general commanding the Grenadiers wore a white (eagle feather) plume on his bearskin and two gold epaulettes. The deputy colonel-general wore a white plume in place of the egret plume and the majors commanding the other regiments of Grenadiers wore two gold epaulettes and a white plume. The major of the 1st Regiment wore a white plume and two gold epaulettes with silver epaulette straps, the Chef de Bataillon one gold epaulette on the left shoulder, one gold contra-epaulette on the right, and a red plume in the bearskin.

Senior officers who were mounted wore high boots of black leather as shown in Fig 26E.

Their horse furniture consisted of a square saddle cloth, crimson for parades and blue for normal wear, white leather French saddle and two tiered pistol hoods. The cloth and hoods were encircled with two lace stripes of gold. The outer being twice the width of the inner. The extreme edge of the hoods and cloth were piped crimson. In the rear quarter a gold crown was set at a 45° angle. On the blue service saddle cloth, gilt grenades may have been used in place of the crown. Black leather rubbing plates appeared beneath the knees of the rider to protect the cloth. Reins and straps were black except for the snaffle bridle and rein which was gold lace covered. The girth and stirrup leathers were white with gilt stirrups. Buckles were gilt. All ranks wore white gloves, cotton for men and thin leather for officers, on parade and in tenue de ville or de sortie.

Some examples of dress are given here, all items being illustrated in colour in Plate 1.

Fig 23. A: Grenadier Consular Guard, grande tenue, 1801-4. Bearskin with cords, habit coat, pouch and sabre briquet, white waistcoat and breeches, white gaiters. B: Grenadier Consular Guard, petit tenue, 1802. Winter-chapeau; surtout, blue trousers, blue waistcoat. Pouch and sabre. C: Summer—as before but white waistcoat, breeches and gaiters. D:

Fig 23

A   B   C

Fig 23

Officer, Grenadiers, 1806-7. Bearskin with cords, surtout (piped red) white waistcoat and breeches. Epée on black waist belt. Boots turned down. E: Grenadier, campaign dress of 1806-7. Bearskin with cords, surtout, white breeches, black gaiters, sabre and pouch belts, pack with chapeau in bag on top of rolled greatcoat. F: Grenadier Officer, tenue de exercise, 1804-9. Chapeau, surtout, blue waistcoat and breeches. Turndown boots. Belt through trouser flap. Fig 24. A: Grenadier, tenue de exercise, 1804-9. Chapeau, surtout, blue waistcoat and breeches. Black gaiters. Full equipment. B: Grenadier at an inspection by the Chefs de Bataillon April 27, 1806. Chapeau, surtout, white waistcoat, fawn breeches, white stockings, buckle shoes. Full equipment. C: Grenadier, tenue de route, 1807. Chapeau with cylindrical plume and tuft. Blue greatcoat with scarlet tabs and white piping on collar, scarlet piping on cuffs. Light blue and white trousers over white gaiters. Bearskin in bag of pack. Full equipment. D: Grenadier, tenue de sortie, summer, 1805-8. Chapeau, habit coat, white waistcoat, fawn breeches, white stockings, buckle shoes, sabre belt only, white gloves. Epée carried on waist belt by NCOs. E: Grenadier, tenue de sortie, winter, 1805-8. As summer example but blue trousers for men. Blue breeches for Corporal and NCO's. Boots 'a la Souvarov' worn by sergeants and corporal. All carried sabre briquet on shoulder belt. F: Grenadier, tenue de sortie, winter. Chapeau, habit coat, white waistcoat, blue breeches, boots 'a la Souvarov', sabre belt. Fig 25. A Grenadier Corporal, tenue d'interieur (winter). Bonnet de police, surtout, white waistcoat, blue breeches, boots 'a la Souvarov'. No equipment. B: Grenadier, tenue de corvee. Bonnet de police, white waistcoat, blue trousers with bottoms rolled up to show white lining, light blue stockings, buckle shoes. C: Grenadier, tenue de corvee. Bonnet de police, surtout, white trousers, brown stockings, buckle shoes. D: Grenadier, tenue de

Fig 24

A B C

D E F

campagne until 1809. Bearskin no plume or cords, surtout, white trousers over white gaiters. Full equipment. Brown gourd on red string over left shoulder. E: Grenadier, tenue de campagne. Bearskin no cords or plume, habit coat, white waistcoat, blue trousers, full equipment. Metal water

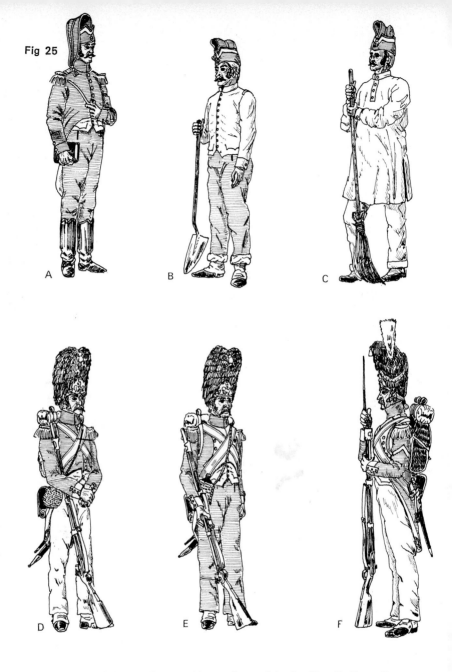

Fig 25

bottle in wicker carrier on white cord over left shoulder. F: Grenadier, re-
turn from Elba 1815. Bearskin with plume and cords, habit coat, white
waistcoat and trousers over white gaiters. Full equipment. Fig 26. A: Velite,
grand tenue, 1804. B: Velite, 1804. Chapeau, surtout, white waistcoat
and breeches. Black gaiters. Full equipment. C: Velite, petit tenue, 1806.

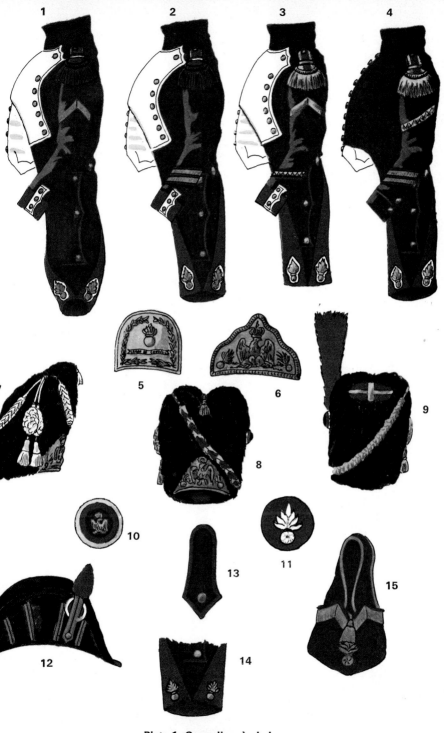

Plate 1: Grenadiers à pied
Key to numbers on page 113

Fig 26

A   B   C   D

Chapeau, surtout, blue waistcoat and breeches. Black gaiters. Sabre belt only D: Velite, grande tenue, 1806. Chapeau with plume, habit coat, white waistcoat, breeches and gaiters. Pouch and sabre. Back pack.

Chasseurs à pied de la Garde 1800-1815

In most respects the Chasseurs followed the Grenadiers in the style and combination of their dress. As with the Grenadiers, the moustache and queue were compulsory.

Headgear

The bearskin worn by the Chasseurs was similar to that worn by the Grenadiers but was minus the plate and cloth patch. The bearskin was encircled by a white plaited cord, which fastened at the right upper side and terminated with two flounders. At the top front of the bearskin there hung two white tassels.

The plume rising from the pom-pon cockade had the lower half green and the upper half scarlet. Until 1806 the cords of the NCOs and fourrier's bearskins was mixed gold and green. In 1807 NCOs and fourriers had their cords in a mixture of red and green, speckled with gold. The tassel above the flounders was mixed gold and green, the tassel on the end of the flounder, mixed scarlet and gold. The flounder itself was interwoven from three cords, scarlet, gold and green. The front top tassels were mixed gold and green. By 1812-13, the cords and plumes were not worn in tenue de route or on campaign (see Plate 2).

Officers, of course, wore the same bearskin with cords and flounders of gold.

The chapeau, again in two styles as with the Grenadiers, was worn for the same occasions. The usual decoration of the chapeau was either a green carrot shaped pom-pon or a similar shape with a tuft. In the latter case the tuft and top half was scarlet, the lower part green. The stiffeners and cockade strap were coloured aurore and the pull tassels green. The stiffeners on the NCO's and fourriers chapeaux were mixed gold and green as were the tassels. The cockade strap was gold.

On the officers' chapeau the stiffeners, tassels and cockade strap were gold. The bonnet de police was identical to that worn by the Grenadiers but in addition an aurore woven hunting horn on a white shaped patch at the front. Epaulettes were worn and were coloured green, lined scarlet with scarlet half moons from 1802-1805. Epaulette loops were green. From 1806 the epaulettes had green straps lined scarlet, scarlet loops and scarlet half moons and fringes.

Coats

The habit coat was identical to that of the Grenadiers except as follows: The white lapels and scarlet cuffs were pointed instead of square. The cuffs were piped white and fastened by two buttons, one above and one on the cuff (Plate 2). The turnbacks and pockets were the same as for the Grenadiers but the turnback ornaments consisted of two horns and two grenades in aurore wool on white patches. The horns appeared on the two outside turnbacks, the grenades on the innermost.

There appears to be good evidence that contrary to the description of the bonnets de police worn by NCOs of the Grenadiers, the bonnets de police of NCOs of the Chasseurs had gold lace and a gold horn, and were piped and tasseled with mixed gold and green.

Corporals had two inverted chevrons of aurore wool, edged scarlet above each cuff. Sergeants had a single gold lace inverted chevron above each cuff, edged scarlet. The epaulette straps were green edged gold, lined scarlet. The half moons were gold. The fringes consisted of one range of red wool, covered by a range of gold. The retaining strap was gold lined scarlet.

Sergeant majors wore two inverted chevrons of gold edged scarlet and epaulettes as for sergeants, the only difference being that in 1806 sergeant majors had two ranges of gold outside the range of scarlet fringes .

Fourriers (quartermasters) were distinguished by the grade stripes of corporals, a gold lace stripe at an angle on each upper arm, lower point to the front. Their epaulettes were as for sergeants. The buttons and turnback ornaments were gold for NCOs and fourriers.

Officers had gilt buttons and gold epaulettes as shown in Appendix 2. The cloth was, of course, of a finer quality. As with the Grenadiers, two habit coats were issued at first, and in 1802 the surtout was introduced

1

2

3

4

5

6

7

8

9

10

11

12

Plate 2: Chasseurs à pied
Key to numbers on page 113

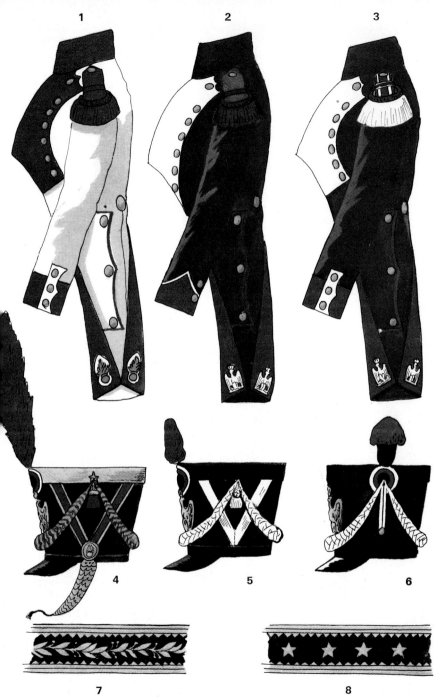

Plate 3: Coat and Facing detail

Habit coats. 1. Grenadiers Hollandais. 2. Fusiliers Chasseurs. 3. Fusiliers Grenadiers.
4. Shako of a Sergeant of Fusiliers Grenadiers. 5. Fusiliers Grenadiers Shako.
6. Early pattern shako of the Fusiliers Chasseurs. 7 and 8. Officers top shako bands.
Left, Fusiliers Chasseurs. Right, Fusiliers Grenadiers.

to take the place of the second habit for petit tenue.

The previous remarks in the section on Grenadiers' surtouts apply equally to those of the Chasseurs, the differences between the two being plain pointed cuffs in place of squared and the use of the horns and grenades on the turnbacks. The surtout was used for petit tenue, tenue de route, and for manoeuvres.

The details of the waistcoat, the sarraut are the same as for the Grenadiers. It would appear that the surtouts were not issued to Chasseurs after 1810 and from that date only used by NCOs.

Details of the overcoat were as for the Grenadiers but no coloured patch appeared. The scarlet piping appears around 1813 on the collar and cuffs. The epaulette loops on the overcoat were first green, then scarlet. In 1814, however, they were blue as the coat.

Legwear and Equipment

This was the same as for the Grenadiers except as follows:

Between 1801-5, the Chasseur sword knot was completely green with a scarlet knot. After this date it was white with a green knot and scarlet tassel. The sword knot of NCOs was green edged gold, the knot was green mixed with gold and the tassel mixed gold and scarlet. The pouch carried a large embossed brass hunting horn on the flap until 1806 when it was replaced by the large crowned eagle. A white cloth cover was often placed over the pouch flap with a black crowned eagle painted in the centre. In the left upper corner was painted a black grenade, a black horn in the right upper, a black grenade in the right lower and a black horn in the left lower corner; see Fig 27D.

Mounted officers were dressed in high boots with saddle cloths and

BELOW: Fig 26. E: Mounted officer of Grenadier à pied. F: Mounted officer of Chasseurs à pied. G: Detail of saddle cloth worn in review order.

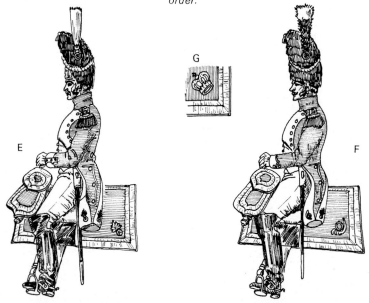

equipment the same as the Grenadiers except that on the blue service saddle cloth, gilt hunting horns appeared. As with the Grenadiers, the senior officers were distinguished as follows:

In the 1st Regiment the colonel-general commanding the Chasseurs wore a white eagle feather plume on his bearskin and two gold epaulettes, the deputy colonel-general wore a white plume in place of the egret plume. The majors commanding the other Chasseur regiments wore two gold epaulettes with silver epaulette straps. The Chefs de Batillon one gold epaulette on the left shoulder, a contra-epaulette on the right, and a green and red plume in the bonnet.

It has been difficult to discover details of the Velites of the Chasseurs and it can only be deduced that they followed the lines laid down by the Grenadier Velites but substituting those details which distinguished Chasseurs from Grenadiers. As is done with the section on the Grenadiers given below is a summary of various orders of dress.

Fig 27. A: Chasseur, full dress, 1801-5. Bearskin with cords, etc, habit coat, white vest, breeches and gaiters. Full equipment. B: Chasseur, tenue de campagne, 1806-7. Bearskin with cords, etc, surtout, white waistcoat and breeches. Black gaiters. Full equipment. Bicorne in bag on rolled greatcoat. C: Chasseur, NCO, tenue de ville. Chapeau, habit coat, white waistcoat, fawn breeches, white stockings, buckle shoes, sabre belt only. D: Chasseur, NCO, tenue de campagne en capote 1813-15. Bearskin without cords or plume, overcoat with piping, blue trousers, full equipment. E: Chasseur, NCO, tenue de route, 1808-9. Chapeau, habit coat, white waistcoat and trousers (over black gaiters) full equipment, Bearskin

Fig 27

A   B   C

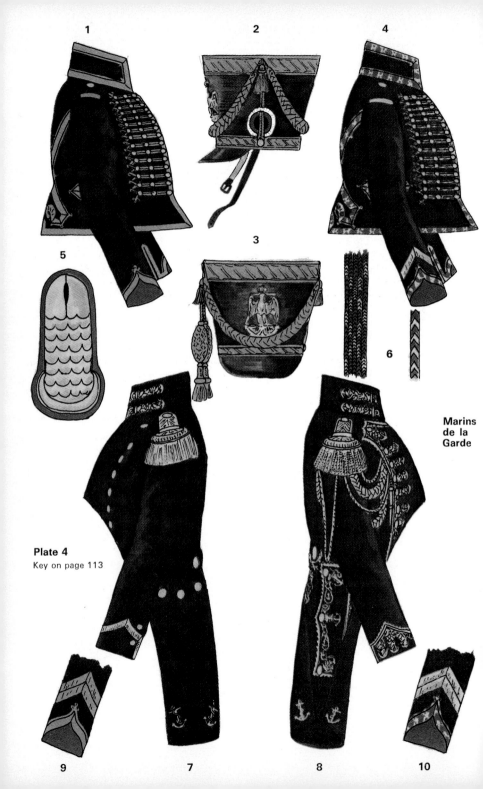

1

2

4

5

3

6

**Marins
de la
Garde**

Plate 4
Key on page 113

9

7

8

10

Plate 5: Coat and Facing detail

Habit coats. 1. Tirailleur Grenadiers. 2. Tirailleur Chasseurs. 3. Voltigeurs.
4. Conscrit Grenadiers. 5. Conscrit Chasseur. 6. Garde National, Voltigeur.

Fig 27

D

E

F

in bag attached at rear of rolled overcoat. F: Chasseur, NCO, tenue de
ville en capote, 1806-12. Chapeau, greatcoat (no piping), boots 'a la
Souvarov', sabre belt only, cream gloves. Fig 28. A: Chasseur, NCO, tenue
de ville, winter, 1810-15. Chapeau, surtout, blue breeches, boots 'a la
Souvarov'. Epée on white waistbelt passing under breeches flap. B:
Chasseur, NCO, with company fanion. C: Chasseur, Officer, grande tenue.

Fig 28

A

B

C

The following points should also be noted:

White trousers were worn in tenue de route in summer, blue in winter. In tenue de ville, the habit coat or surtout was worn; in summer, with white waistcoats, breeches and stockings with buckle shoes and in winter, with blue waistcoat and breeches and boots 'a la Souvarov'. In rain the greatcoat was worn. Tenue de corvee or fatigues was the same as for the Grenadiers.

Grenadiers Hollandais

The Grenadiers Hollandais wore an identical style uniform to the Grenadiers à pied Francais, but with various colour differences described below.

Head-dress

The bearskins did not have a front plate, but retained the 'fond' or patch at the top. Cords were white and the patch was crimson with a white grenade. A scarlet plume rose from a pom-pon cockade on the left side. An interesting point is the use by the Grenadiers Hollandais, of white metal or brass chin scales (see Fig 28 E/F). NCOs had mixed scarlet and gold cords and a gold grenade on the patch. Officers had gold cords and a gold patch grenade. The chapeau was identical with the later model used by the Grenadiers and conformed in respect of colouring for the different ranks. The field service cap was white with crimson lace and piping. The hair was worn in a queue and powdered. Moustaches were compulsory for men and NCOs.

Coats

As part of the Dutch Guard, the uniform was as follows: A white habit coat was worn with collar, square lapels, cuffs, turnbacks, and the piping of the pockets, all crimson. The button holes of the lapels and pockets were decorated with white lace brandenbergs as were the collars. In French service the uniform remained the same but brandenbergs were not used.

The epaulettes and retaining loops were scarlet and aurore grenades on white patches appeared on the turnbacks. Buttons were all brass. For service and undress wear a white surtout, in the style of the Grenadiers Francais, was worn with the collar, cuffs, turnbacks and pocket piping in crimson. Waistcoats and breeches were white and the gaiters white for summer and parade wear, black for service and winter wear.

The greatcoat was the same style as the Grenadiers. Authorities vary on the colour of the greatcoat but we can assume that light blue grey was the regulation wear with steel grey or dark blue being used when the other colour was unobtainable. There appears to have been scarlet piping on the collar and cuffs of the light blue coat.

Officers followed the same pattern as the Grenadiers Francais except, of course, that the colours were white and crimson. The collar, lapels,

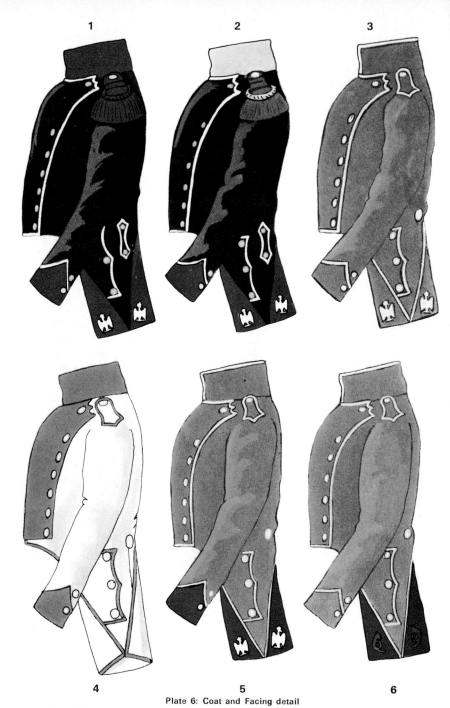

Plate 6: Coat and Facing detail

1. Habit veste worn by Tirailleurs after 1812. 2. Habit veste, Voltigeurs. 3. Habit veste in the regulation colours of the Pupilles de la Garde, 4. Habit coat worn by the Pupilles under Dutch regulations. This continued in wear under the French. The facing colours varied greatly. 5. Habit veste, Flanqueur Grenadiers. 6 Habit veste, Flanqueur-Chasseurs.

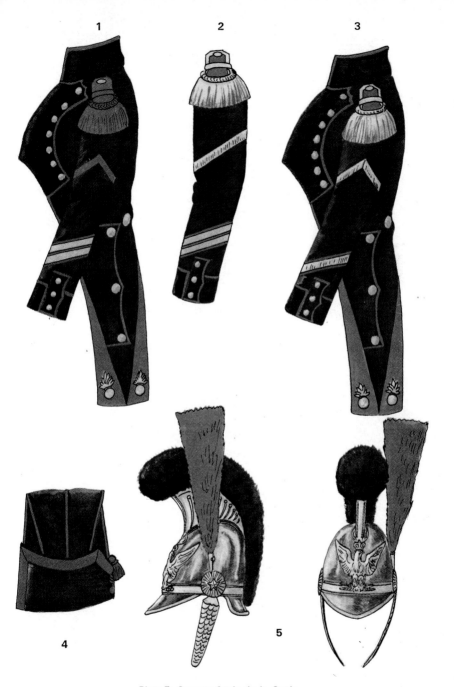

Plate 7: Sapeurs Genie de la Garde
1. Habit coat, Sapeur Caporal. 2. Fourrier's sleeve detail. 3. Habit coat of Sergeant.
4. Sapeur Bonnet de Police. 5. Helmet of the Sapeurs Genie.

ABOVE: A Grenadier of the Royal Dutch Guard; note the lace brandenbergs on the collar and lapels. (Collection of Colonel Druene).

cuffs and cuff slashes were of crimson velvet and in some cases the turnbacks were white with gold embroidered eagles decorating them. This is believed to have been the full dress uniform and for service wear a coat identical to the men's was worn with the addition of gilt buttons and being made of a finer quality cloth.

Fig 28

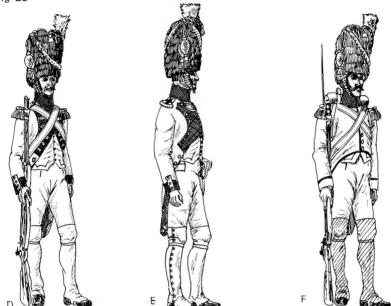

ABOVE: D: Grenadier, Dutch Royal Guard. E: Grenadier Hollandais, officer, full dress. F: Grenadier Hollandais, petite tenue.

Legwear and Equipment

This was the same as the Grenadiers Francais but the pouch was embossed only with a copper eagle. In tenue de campagne a white cloth cover was carried on the flap upon which was painted a yellow eagle.

Fusiliers Chasseurs

The regiment of Fusiliers Chasseurs wore an almost identical uniform to that of the Chasseurs à pied. The only difference in the habit coat from that of the Chasseurs, was the use of blue, piped scarlet, shoulder straps and white cloth eagles on the turnbacks. The buttons were of brass. Around the beginning of 1809, epaulettes with green shoulder straps and scarlet half moons and fringes were introduced. The retaining straps were scarlet. The shako first used was the light infantry model. A single white plaited cord hung across the front with a single flounder on the right side. The gusset into which the pom-pon or plume was fixed was on the left side and covered by a tricolour cockade.

A white 'ganse' or cockade strap passed over the cockade, buttoning below. In many instances this strap is not shown by contemporary prints. From 1810 the cockade and plume moved to the front of the shako in the normal fashion. From 1809, brass chinscales were worn, previously there was no method of securing the shako to the wearer's head. The sabre knot was white with a green knot and scarlet tassels. Corporals were

Plate 8: Sapeur, Grenadiers à pied, Full dress uniform

distinguished by two aurore wool inverted chevrons above each cuff. Sous officers, sergeants and sergeant majors, came from the Old Guard and retained on their turnbacks gold grenades and horns at first. Later white eagles were displayed. Rank distinctions and epaulettes were identical to those of the Chasseurs à pied. The cordons of NCOs shakos were mixed scarlet, green and gold. Some sources refer to the shakos of NCOs having a gold lace band at the top and sergeant majors having a narrower one below it. The eagle and chin straps were also gold. The pouch flap was decorated by a brass crowned eagle. Officers wore identical uniforms to the Chasseurs à pied with the exception of the shakos.

The top band of the officers' shako was in black velvet edged with narrow gold piping. On the band, laurel leaves appeared (see Plate 3). Cords, eagle plate, chin straps and metal edging to the peak were gold. The cockade strap and tulip holder were also gold. The bottom band was in many cases edged top and bottom with gold. The red tipped, green plume rose from a gilt tulip shaped holder as mentioned above. Senior officers, the colonel and major, had a white plume.

The field service caps for both the Fusiliers Chasseurs and the Fusiliers Grenadiers were identical to both regiments.

There does exist, however, some uncertainty as to the colours used. From Bucquoy we find the lacing and piping scarlet. Rousselot, however, shows aurore. The basic colour of the Field Service cap was blue and was in the Dragoon style.

Unless specifically mentioned in the foregoing, the equipment was identical to that described for the Grenadiers à pied. The musket was almost identical but usually had white metal bands. The hair was sometimes worn in a queue and powdered. Moustaches were compulsory for men and NCOs. These regulations were relaxed very quickly and short hair was usually worn. Moustaches also seemed to be a matter of personal preference.

Fusiliers Grenadiers

This regiment, again, had a similar uniform with only relatively small differences. The shako at first appears to be the 1806 model and at least one contemporary source shows it with a white lace top band, white lace on the stiffeners and white cords and flounders. At the front a brass eagle plate was worn beneath a tricolour cockade which was held in place by a white 'ganse'. A scarlet carrot shaped pom-pon was carried above the cockade. The coat shown in the print is very interesting in that red piping appears on the collar and lapels. In other respects the coat was similar to the Grenadier's coat except that the cuffs are shown piped white as were the scarlet three pointed cuff flaps and the scarlet turnbacks. Pointed shoulder straps were worn with the aforementioned uniform either blue piped scarlet (1806-7) or scarlet piped white (1807-8).

The more well-known uniform was indeed identical to that worn by the Grenadiers à pied with the following differences. From 1808 full epaulettes had scarlet straps with two white laces along their length, white or scarlet half moons, both colours appear in prints and the fringes

Fig 29

were white. No decoration appears on the turnbacks until around 1808 when white eagles appeared. From 1806-9 the shako was as already described. But in 1809 the top lace band was discontinued. From this time the carrot shaped pom-pon was replaced by a scarlet plume without a ball. As with the Fusiliers Chasseurs brass chin scales appear after 1809. Between 1812-14, a scarlet lentile disc was worn in place of the plume. During the campaign of 1807 fawn/brown trousers were worn over white gaiters. On this campaign at least, no plume, pom-pons or cords were worn and the top white lace band is not evident. A brass crowned eagle decorated the pouch flap and in all other respects equipment followed the lines of the Grenadiers à pied.

A Fusilier Grenadier in tenue de ville around 1808 is shown wearing a chapeau identical to that worn by the Grenadiers à pied and one therefore concludes that this headgear was issued to the Fusiliers. The figure in question wears in addition the habit coat, white waistcoat and fawn/ brown trousers. The sabre briquet was carried on the shoulder belt. White trousers were in use in 1811 and blue trousers from 1812-13. A

OPPOSITE PAGE: A: Fusilier Chasseur, 1807-8. B: Fusilier Chasseur, 1809. C: Fusilier Chasseur, full dress, 1809-10. D: Fusilier Chasseur, full dress, 1810-14. E: Fusilier Chasseur in barrack dress. F: Fusilier Chasseur, officer. BELOW: A: Fusilier Grenadier, 1806-7. Note this dress had red piping to the collar and lapels, white piping to cuffs and flaps, and blue shoulder straps piped red. B: Fusilier Grenadier, 1807-8. As previous figure but in this case the shoulder straps were red piped white. C: Fusilier Grenadier Officer.

Fig 30

A   B   C

Fig 30

D   E   F

ABOVE: D: Fusilier Grenadier in tenue de route 1813-14. E: Fusilier Grenadier NCO. F: Fusilier Grenadier in tenue de ville.

blue greatcoat was used during the first years, giving way to a steel grey greatcoat in 1811. Also from this time, and probably before, oilskin covers appeared over the shakos in tenue de marche and in bad weather. The sabre knots were white with scarlet knots and tassels. Corporals wore two aurore wool stripes, angled above each cuff. The epaulettes of the sergeants and fourriers were the same as the mens but with half moons of gold. Sergeant majors had additionally a range of gold fringes over the white fringes. The chevrons on the shakos of sergeants, fourriers and sergeant majors were scarlet edged with gold and the top band was covered with gold lace. It is possible that the sergeant majors had an additional narrower gold band beneath the gold lace top band. Cords and flounders were mixed gold and scarlet. The NCOs sabre knot was white with mixed scarlet and gold tassels and knots.

The remarks regarding officers in the Fusiliers Chasseurs is equally applicable to those of the Fusiliers Grenadiers. The differences apart from the turnback ornaments was in the shako top band. Also in some instances the white lace chevrons appeared on officers' shakos but this does not appear to be the general rule. In the case of the Fusiliers Grenadiers, this was again of black velvet piped with narrow gold bands but in place of the laurel leaves there appeared gold stars (see Plate 3). The plume was scarlet in a gold tulip holder and white for senior officers. Equipment was as detailed for the Fusiliers Chasseurs. Hair was worn in a queue and moustaches were worn.

Velites of Florence and Turin

These two units wore an identical uniform to the Fusiliers Grenadiers.

Company of Veterans

The Company of Veterans wore almost identical uniforms to the Grenadiers à pied but with red lapels and blue cuff flaps in place of the white items on the Grenadiers uniform. The chapeau was worn in place of the bearskin, with a scarlet carrot shaped pom-pon. Also the pocket flaps were horizontal instead of vertical but again piped scarlet. Hair was worn in a queue and powdered. Moustaches were compulsory.

Marins or Matelots de la Garde

This unit wore one of the most unusual uniforms for a foot unit in the whole Grande Armée. Only the officers wore anything resembling what we may term the standard style of dress. It is felt that readers will find these uniforms of great interest so they are described in detail below.

Head-dress

In 1804 when the unit was formed a shako similar to the light infantry model was worn. The varnished leather peak was attached by means of hooks and eyes just above the lower band. The top band was covered by aurore lace, 40 mm wide and the lower band by aurore lace 34 mm wide. A tricolour cockade was fixed at the top front by a 'V' shaped 'ganse' or aurore cord. This fastened to a small uniform button at the base of the 'V'. Across the front of the shako hung a single aurore coloured cord, below which hung a plaited aurore cord. On the right side a tassel and on the left two flounders hung, all coloured aurore. For full dress a scarlet plume (without a ball) was worn, while for service wear a scarlet carrot shaped pom-pon was worn.

In 1808 a second model shako was introduced which was essentially the same as for the former model. The two bands of aurore lace remained. Now, however, the plaited aurore cord hung front and rear and the flounders hung from the right. At the front appeared a brass stamped eagle superimposed over an anchor. The tricolour cockade now appeared at the lower left side above the bottom band. A double aurore cord dropped vertically from the top band, passed under the cockade, through the cockade below the first white ring, over the remainder of the cockade to fasten to a small uniform button placed on the lower band. The peak was again removable and fastened in the same manner and place as on the first model.

Early in 1809 yet another model was introduced. This model was higher and had a more pronounced bell shaped configuration (see Plate 4). The peak was now fixed in place at the bottom of the shako front and a black leather chin strap was worn which had a small brass buckle on the left side. The cordons, lace bands and the eagle plate were identical to the second model. The scarlet plume was worn for full dress wear and an aurore or scarlet carrot shaped pom-pon was worn for service attire. In 1809 a dull black cover was worn over the shako for tenue de route and from 1810 a black oilskin cover.

The sous officers, contre maitres (sergeants) and maitres (sergeant majors) had gold lace on the top and bottom bands of their shakos. Cord and flounders were mixed scarlet and gold with a ratio of two scarlet to one gold. The eagle and anchor plate was yellow brass.

The bonnet de police of the men was blue with aurore lace and piping. At the front an aurore anchor was worn. The sous officers had a bonnet de police with gold lace and anchor. The piping and tassel was mixed scarlet and gold to the ratio already given.

Sous officers, and possibly the men, wore in some instances a chapeau for tenue de ville. This was identical to that worn by the Grenadiers à pied and in the case of the sous officers had gold stiffeners and gold cockade strap. The tassels were mixed scarlet and gold. The chapeau was probably worn without a pom-pon but possibly a scarlet shaped pom-pon appeared.

Officers would appear to have worn chapeaux, usually in the fore and aft position, and these varied in style. Examples are given in Fig 32 but the following details were applicable to any style: Black with gold stiffeners and cockade strap. Gold tassel pulls were also in evidence.

On campaign no plume or pom-pon was carried but otherwise a scarlet plume was worn. Senior officers, capitaines de vaisseaus, wore a white plume. The bonnets de police of the officers were blue with the lace and piping all gold.

Other Ranks' Dress

The basic item of wear was called a 'paletot' which was in point of fact a blue Hussar style dolman. Down the chest there were fifteen horizontal rows of double braid, aurore for the men and quartier-maitres (who were later referred to also as corporals) and mixed scarlet and gold (2:1) for sous officers (see Plate 4).

The braid formed trefoils or 'crows feet' at the top and bottom edges and looped between rows. On the right hand side were two vertical rows of buttons and on the left, one. From 1809 there were three rows of buttons on the right side and two on the left. As will be seen in Section 4, the trumpeters and drummers had this type of dolman from their inception. Loops on the left inner edge fastened over the buttons on the right inner side. Very often only the top three loops, which were longer than the others, were fastened, showing the waistcoat beneath.

The blue collar was laced aurore on all edges, inside which a very narrow piping in aurore appeared. On each shoulder an aurore loop or strap appeared, together with a small uniform button near the collar.

The front and bottom edges were lace aurore. The back seams were also laced aurore with the piping on either side. Three different styles are shown in Fig 33. Lace and piping also appeared at each side of the dolman in a double spearhead design. The pointed cuffs were scarlet, laced aurore. Note that where aurore lace or piping is attributed to the

---

Fig 31

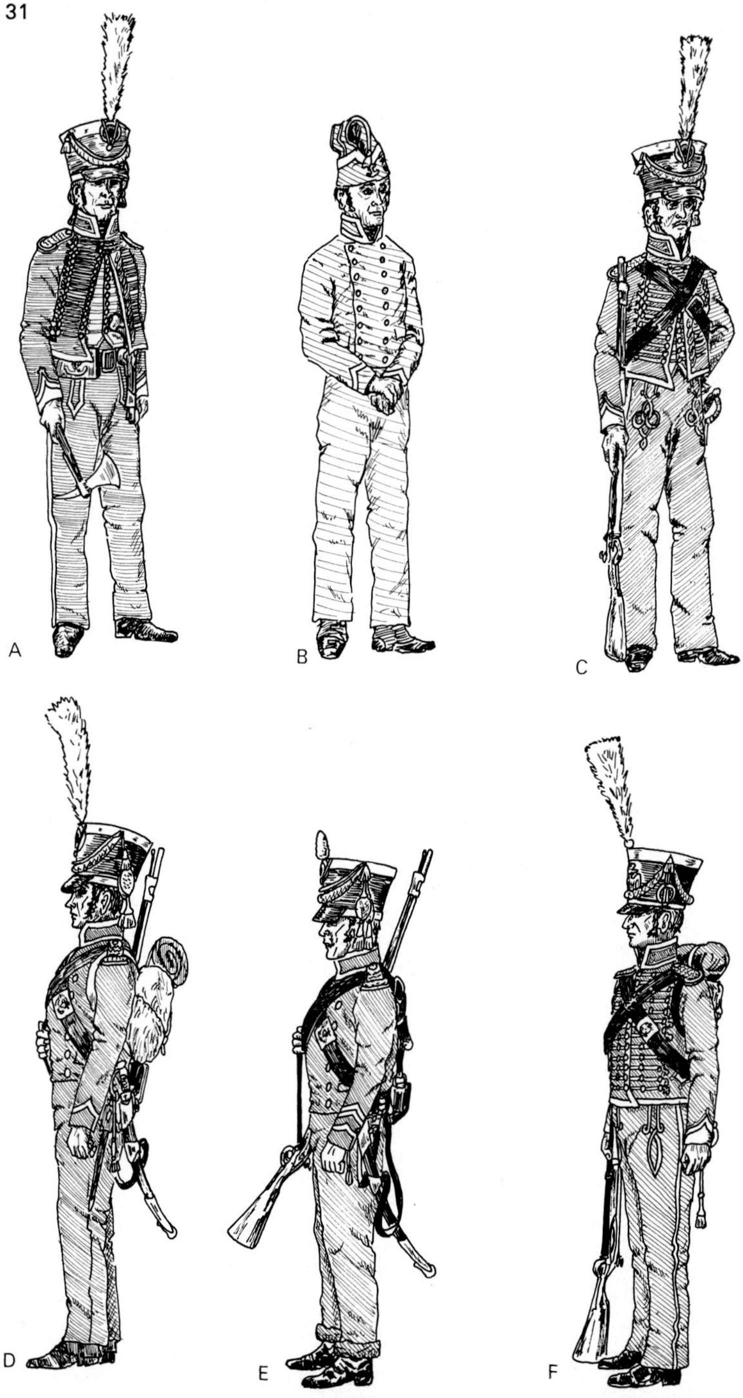

A   B   C

D   E   F

55

men, the sous officers had mixed scarlet and gold. Details of the form the mixed lace and piping took is shown in Plate 4. On the shoulder brass scale straps were worn on a scarlet lining. The form is shown in Plate 4. The buttons were domed and under the Garde des Consuls carried an anchor with a bundle of rods (lictors fascine) superimposed. The initials RF appeared, one on either side and around the circumference the words 'Garde des Consuls'. As part of the Garde Imperial a crowned eagle appeared (see Fig 33).

The trousers were blue with aurore (mixed gold and scarlet for sous officers) stripes on the outside seams and either spearheads or Hungarian knots at the fronts depending on the period. Under the Garde des Consuls a simple spearhead appeared. In 1806 Hungarian knots replaced the spearheads. These were modified to a simpler style in 1811; see Fig 33. Black leather boots of Hussar style but without edging or tassels were worn under the trousers for full dress wear. For service wear they were replaced by shoes and grey or black gaiters in the winter and white in the summer. White gaiters were also worn on campaign.

A figure in the collection of Raoul and Jean Brunon shows a quartier-maitre wearing Hungarian breeches with the side stripe looping over the seat. Both the Hungarian knots and the striping were edged with 'soutaches', narrow piping with loops. It is difficult to decide on the authenticity of this garment but to the modeller offers an unusual figure (Fig 32A).

Beneath the dolman all ranks wore a scarlet waistcoat braided in aurore for the men and mixed scarlet and gold for the sous officers. It was edged with the appropriate lace and there were three rows of fifteen brass or gold buttons. For service wear a blouse, known as a 'caracot' was worn, (see Fig 32D). This was a blue waist length jacket with two vertical rows of eight buttons and fastened on the right side. The collar and pointed cuffs were laced aurore as was the loop on the shoulder. At each side, just above the bottom edge, was a strap with a buckle to adjust the fit. The brass shoulder scales were worn with the 'caracot'. Normal legwear with the 'caracot' was a pair of plain blue trousers, sometimes the bottoms rolled up to the ankles. Gaiters, white or grey, were worn under the trousers. A blue overcoat was worn reaching to just below the knee. It was double breasted and fastened at the right. There were two rows of seven uniform buttons down the front and one at each end of a half belt at the back. The cuffs were round and the brass shoulder scales were worn on the greatcoat.

Officers' Dress

In theory the officers of the Marins de la Garde were dressed in the same manner as their counterparts in the Navy. That is with a variable number of gold laces across the chest (Fig 34C).

In practice various styles were worn, the head wear having been des-

---

OPPOSITE PAGE: A: Quartier-Maitre in tenue de ville. B: Marin, full dress 1813. C: Marin, tenue de campagne in greatcoat. D: Marin, tenue de campagne, 1812-14. E: Maitre in tenue de ville, 1803. F: Lieutenant de vaisseau, 1810.

Fig 32

A   B   C

D   E   F

cribed above. The dress of around 1805 appears as a blue surtout, fastened with seven gold buttons. The collar was edged top and bottom with gold braid as were the pointed cuffs. On the blue turnbacks appeared gold anchors. The epaulette on the left and the contra epaulette and aiguilette on the right shoulder followed the standard method of indicating rank. The waistcoat which showed plainly beneath the surtout was white. Over the waistcoat, either a plain white or a black edged gold waist belt was worn. The belt fastened by a plate carrying the eagle and anchor insignia in various forms.

In full dress the light epée sword was sometimes carried at first but the normal weapon was a light cavalry sabre. The epée was retained for tenue de ville. Hussar breeches were worn, blue with the standard gold lace spearhead rank markings and gold lace stripe. Hussar boots with gold edging and tassels were worn.

By 1807 a habit coat appears to have been adopted. Here there would appear to be two forms. One with gold embroidery across the chest etc, and the other, simpler, with or without gold piping to the lapels for petite tenue or service wear (Fig 34A). This is a difficult point as we know that the surtout was worn on campaign and probably also in petite tenue. It is probable that the individual officer decided which style he used. The habit coat worn for full dress had pointed lapels and cuffs. The coat was entirely blue and it is noted that in some examples, as, as with the Hussar officers in petit tenue, the lapel tops were not the ecusson shape but rounded; (Fig 34C).

On the collar at each side appeared two strips of embroidered gold leaves atop an anchor. The lapels were either edged with gold piping or had embroidered stripes, similar to the collar bars, placed horizontally across from the button holes. Epaulettes and aiguilettes remained standard. The cuffs were edged with gold lace and on the horizontal pocket flaps were three button laces. Gold anchors appeared on the plain turnbacks. The full dress waistcoat was scarlet with five rows of buttons and braided with gold. Hussar style boots and breeches were worn as already described.

The second style (petit tenue) was similar but with only the embroidery on the collar and lacing on the cuffs. The anchors of course appeared on the turnbacks. The remainder of the uniform remained the same, ie, waistcoat, breeches and boots.

The black, gold edged, belt now appeared as standard with the single bar hilt sabre in a black leather scabbard with gold mounts and heel. Steel scabbards with gold mounts were also used.

The surtout continued to be worn on campaign, with seven to nine buttons at the front and with the same embellishments as already described for the uniform of 1805. The waistcoat was white or blue. Pantalons à cheval or over trousers of blue and without any leather lining were sometimes worn. These buttoned on the outside seams by 18 gold buttons.

OPPOSITE PAGE: A: Belt and scabbard variations of the Marins. B: Sabre briquet peculiar to the Marins. C: Button of the Marins in the Consular Guard. D: Buttons of the Marins in the Imperial Guard. E: Pouch of the Marins. F: Small pouch worn on the waist belt by Marins of the Consular Guard. G and H: Variations in thigh ornaments J: Detail of the aurore shako lace. K: Shako plate of the Marins. L: Various styles of back seam ornamentation. M: Embossed belt plate.

Fig 33

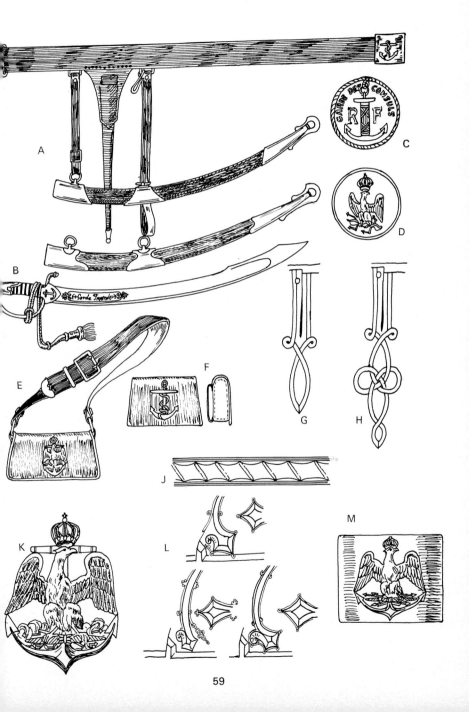

A riding coat or frock coat was worn by officers for tenue de ville, and a cloak was also worn in inclement weather; both were blue.

All officers were mounted and used a blue French saddle on a blue square horse cloth edged with gold lace. In the rear corners appeared an embroidered gold eagle. The pistol hoods were triple tiered with gold or blue lace. The girth was blue. The remainder of the straps were of black leather but senior officers had a gold snaffle bridle and rein. The commandant of the corps, either an admiral or a capitaine de vaisseau had a crimson saddle cloth. Senior officers had an additional gold stripe inside and half the width of the outer.

Equipment

When formed as part of the Consular Guard, the armament of the Marins was most unusual. The first rank of a battalion was armed with a sabre, the second rank with an axe and the third rank with a pike. All carried a pistol thrust into their waistbelt. The sabre was carried on a black belt over the right shoulder.

In 1805 the Marins were issued with muskets, bayonets and a short sabre, similar to the sabre briquet. Until 1805, a black leather waist belt, with a large brass buckle at the front, was worn. Attached to the belt at the right front was a small pouch with a brass anchor on the flap (see Fig 33F).

The calf skin pack was suspended by black leather straps although a figure dated 1806 shows white. As with so many items, when on cam-

---

BELOW: A: Enseigne de vaisseau on campaign, 1807. B: Enseigne—full dress, 1805. C: Detail of the uniform of a capitaine de vaisseau, 1813-14.

Fig 34

A   B   C

paign normal replacements were not always available and it is probable that this is the reason for the different colour.

From 1805 a larger pouch (see Fig 33E) was carried on a black leather shoulder belt, over the left shoulder, which passed over the sabre belt. This belt was fastened by a brass buckle in the same manner as cavalry pouches.

On campaign a cover was placed over the pouch to protect the brass eagle anchor. It is difficult to find any reference to the exact form this took, but following normal practice one can suggest it was of white cloth with the eagle/anchor design painted on in black.

Around 1805-06 the large buckle, evident on the waist belt previously, was replaced by an oblong plate of brass bearing an embossed anchor.

The sabre, in a black leather scabbard, was hung from two black leather straps which attached to two rings sewn into the belt. Between these rings the bayonet frog was sewn.

The sabre was somewhat different from the infantry sabre briquet and is shown in Fig 33B. Note that in place of the flat woven sword knot used by the infantry, a cord style was used and was coloured aurore.

With all the leather equipment, the Marin had two sets. One varnished for full dress wear and one left soft and supple for normal wear. The bayonet was carried in a black leather scabbard with a brass heel and the musket was bound in brass with a sling of black leather.

The sabre incidentally was usually worn with the top swivel carrying ring hung on to a hook attached to the belt. The blade of the sabre was in most cases engraved as shown in Fig 33B.

The greatcoat was rolled and strapped (with black leather straps) to the top of the pack.

Tirailleurs Grenadiers

The Tirailleurs Grenadiers were the first regiment of the Jeune Guard (Young Guard) and the first regiment of the Guard in which is found the beginning of a more modern uniform (see Fig 36A).

Headgear

The shako was the normal 1809 style with white lace chevrons at the sides. At the front a brass eagle plate was carried beneath the tricolour cockade. The plume was scarlet over white in equal proportions and had a pom-pon at the base. The cords and flounders were white. Brass chin scales were worn and the peak edged with brass. On service the plume was replaced by a pom-pon. For the first regiment the pom pon below the plume and the pom-pon worn by itself was red over white. For the second regiment, white over red. Cords were usually dispensed with on service.

Sergeants and sergeant majors had the chevrons on their shakos of red lace edged with gold. The cords and flounders were mixed gold and red in the proportion of 1:2. Officers had gold lace chevrons and gold cords and flounders. Around the top of the shako was a black velvet band, edged with gold and with gold stars between, as described for the Fusiliers Grenadiers.

A scarlet plume was carried in a gilt tulip holder. The plume was white for the colonel and major.

Coats

The men wore a blue habit coat with pointed lapels and pointed cuffs. This coat differed from the habit coats used by the previous regiments in that the coat tails were very much shorter. The collar was red, piped with blue. The pointed lapels were blue piped white. The vertical pockets were outlined with white piping and the red turnbacks were ornamented with white wool eagles. Pointed shoulder straps were worn and were red, edged with white piping as were the red pointed cuffs. All the buttons were brass.

Corporals were distinguished by two aurore coloured inverted chevrons above each cuff. The sergeants and sergeant majors were distinguished respectively by one or two gold lace inverted chevrons above each cuff. Additionally the sous officers wore epaulettes with white shoulder straps carrying two thin gold lines, gold half moons and the fringes were mixed white and gold. The turnbacks eagles were also gold.

All ranks carried steel grey overcoats. The coats of the officers were identical to those worn by officers of the Fusiliers Grenadiers.

The men and NCOs wore white waistcoats and breeches with short, below the knee gaiters, which had brass buttons. On service and in tenue de route white or blue trousers were worn.

The sword knot was white with a red knot and tassel. All other equipment was identical to that carried by the Fusiliers and Grenadiers. The

---

BELOW: Young Guard in Spain. A: Voltigeur wearing standard coat, fawn trousers. The pouch has a white cover with a yellow eagle painted on it. The pom-pon is green. B: Tirailleur in grey greatcoat. Trousers are blue with red piping. C: Tirailleur in dark brown greatcoat piped red on collar (including the tab), shoulder straps, cuffs and front of coat. Trousers are blue with red piping. Red pom-pon of unusual shape and a yellow eagle painted on oilskin cover.

Fig 35

A   B   C

mounted officers had a crimson saddle cloth, edged with gold and with a white leather French saddle. Long riding boots with knee guards were worn by mounted officers.

Tirailleurs Chasseurs

The uniform of the Tirailleurs Chasseurs was identical to that worn by the Tirailleurs Grenadiers except as detailed below (see Plates 5 and 6).

The pointed shoulder straps in this case were green with red, sometimes shown white, piping. The turnback ornaments consisted of green eagles and hunting horns. The eagles appearing on the two outermost turnbacks and the horns on the two innermost. The plume or pom-pon was green. Corporals were distinguished in the same manner as for the Tirailleurs Grenadiers. Sergeants and sergeant majors also had the same rank markings as the Tirailleurs Grenadiers but with the shako cords and flounders mixed green and gold. In some cases the NCOs shakos were further ornamented with a narrow gold piping around the top of the shako. The NCOs epaulettes had the fringes mixed green and gold in place of white and gold. Otherwise they were identical to the epaulettes of the Tirailleurs Grenadiers. The turnback eagles and horns were gold.

The equipment was the same as for the Tirailleurs Grenadiers but the sabre knots were all white.

The officers were dressed the same as the officers of the Fusiliers Chasseurs.

Conscrits Grenadiers

The uniforms of the Conscrits Grenadiers was a mixture of the types already described (see Plate 5). The shako was identical to that worn by the Tirailleurs Grenadiers but with the red plume for full dress, no pom-pon, and a red pom-pon for service wear. Cords and flounders were red and the peak was not edged with brass.

The short tailed coat had a plain blue collar, plain blue square cut lapels piped white and blue pointed shoulder straps piped red. The cuffs were red with a white three pointed cuff slash. The turnbacks were white, piped red with red cloth eagles. The vertical pockets were piped red. The remainder of the uniform, breeches, equipment, etc, was the same as for the Tirailleur Grenadiers.

The differences in rank were identical to the Tirailleurs Grenadiers but with angled stripes above each cuff. Officers' uniforms were again identical to those of the Tirailleurs Grenadiers.

Conscrits Chasseurs

The Conscrits Chasseurs wore an identical uniform to the Tirailleurs Chasseurs but with blue turnbacks piped red (see Fig 36D). Turnback horns were white. All other details were as for the Tirailleurs Chasseurs.

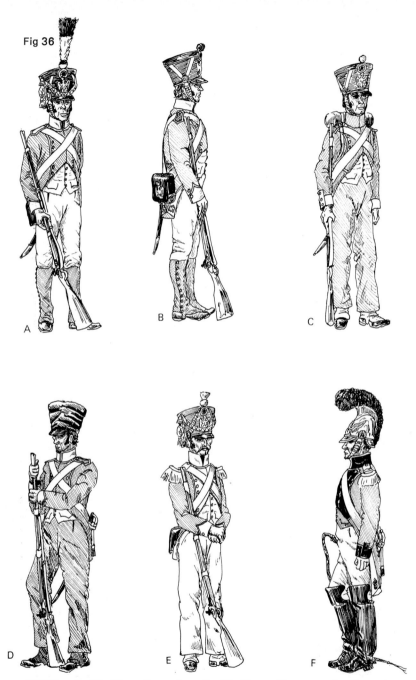

Fig 36

A

B

C

D

E

F

ABOVE: A: Tirailleur Grenadier. B: Tirailleur Chasseur. C: Conscrit Grenadier. D: Conscrit Chasseur, tenue de campagne. E: Grenadier, Garde National de la Garde. F: Driver of the Sapeurs-Genie.

Gardes Nationales de la Garde

This regiment wore a very similar uniform to the line regiments and was organised on their pattern. That is with flank or élite companies, Grenadiers and Voltigeurs and the majority of centre companies, Fusiliers.

The basic uniform consisted of a blue coat with short tails and pointed lapels and cuffs. The collars were red, piped white as were the cuffs. The lapels and turnbacks were white, piped red. The vertical pockets were piped white (see Fig 36E).

A white waistcoat and white breeches were worn. The black gaiters were long as worn by the Grenadiers à pied. It was more usual to see the Natioinal Guard wearing white or blue trousers. In common with other regiments of the Young Guard the musket was bound throughout with iron. Otherwise the equipment was as described for the Fusiliers Grenadiers.

The differences between Grenadiers, Voltigeurs and Fusiliers were as follows: Grenadiers wore a shako, plain black without any edging to the peak, with a brass eagle plate at the front and brass chin scales. Cords and flounders were red and a red tufted pom-pon was worn. Sword knot was white with a red knot and tassel. Red epaulettes were worn, and red grenades appeared on the turnbacks.

Voltigeurs wore the same shako but with green cords, flounders and tufted pom-pon. Epaulettes were green as were the knot and tassel on the sword knot. Green horns appeared on the turnbacks. Fusiliers again wore the same shako but with white cords and flounders. Either a lentile disc or a tufted pom-pon was worn in the following company colours. Green for the 1st company, deep skyblue for the 2nd, aurore for the 3rd and violet for the 4th company. Pointed shoulder straps were worn of blue piped red. The turnbacks carried blue eagles. Sword knot was plain white.

The corporal as was normal, wore the same uniform as the men but with the addition of two aurore wool, inverted chevrons above each cuff.

Sergeants and sergeant majors had one or two gold lace chevrons respectively above each cuff.

Epaulettes were worn by NCOs with gold lace edged straps (red for Grenadiers and green for Voltigeurs) gold half moons and mixed green and gold fringes for the Voltigeurs and mixed red and gold for the Grenadiers. Fusilier sergeants probably wore the same shoulder straps as the men. Shako cords and flounders were mixed red and gold for Grenadier NCOs, green and gold for Voltigeurs, NCOs and white and gold for Fusilier NCOs. The NCOs shakos probably had a gold lace band around the top. The appropriate turnback ornaments were gold.

Officers wore the same uniform as the Tirailleurs Chasseurs but with the plume red over green in equal proportions.

Sapeurs du Genie de la Garde

While not strictly infantry, the Sapeurs du Genie de la Garde consisted mainly of foot soldiers and wore a most unusual uniform as described in the following section.

Head-dress

The Old Guard section wore a white metal helmet almost identical to that worn by the Regiments of Carbiniers. The front and rear peaks were edged with yellow brass (as opposed to the usual brass which had a distinct copper colour) and a yellow brass strip encircled the bottom of the helmet.

A decorated yellow brass 'comb' was rivetted to the top part and on the comb was a black crest. The front of the helmet bore a yellow brass eagle which had the wings extended upwards instead of as usual in the Napoleonic style coming downwards. Large circular rosaces with a five pointed star in the centre appeared at each side and yellow brass chin scales hung from these. Above the left hand rosace a yellow brass plume holder, with a small screw to hold the plume in place was fixed. For full dress wear a scarlet plume was worn (see Plate 7).

The only difference between officers and men was the use of gilt in place of yellow brass, and a gilt tulip holder for the plume. The senior officer commanding the company and later the battalion wore a white plume.

The sapeurs 1st, and later, 2nd class, of the Old Guard company (as well as all the corporals and NCOs) wore this helmet. Later when sapeurs 3rd class or Young Guard were introduced they wore the shako which was basically as already described, being the 1807 model with a plain peak. Chin scales were of yellow brass as was the normal style eagle plate at the front (see Fig 37E).

Scarlet cords and flounders were worn together with a scarlet plume and pom-pon for full dress occasions. For tenue ordinaire only a scarlet pom-pon appeared. The field service cap or bonnet de police was blue with scarlet lace and piping. A scarlet grenade was worn at the front.

NCOs had gold lace and mixed red and gold piping and tassel on their bonnet de police. A gold grenade appeared at the front. Officers had all lace and piping in gold.

In tenue de route and for service wear the officers normally wore a chapeau with gold cockade strap, stiffeners and pull tassels. A plume does not appear to have been worn.

Coats

The coat worn by both the Old and Young Guard contingents was identical and was basically the same as the Grenadiers of the Old Guard with colour differences.

The coat was blue with a black velvet cuff, cuff flaps, lapels (square cut) and collar. All of which were piped scarlet. The turnbacks were scarlet with aurore grenade ornaments fastened directly to the turnbacks and not having white patches as did the Grenadiers of the Old Guard.

The vertical pockets were piped scarlet. Buttons were of yellow brass. Scarlet epaulettes were worn and the retaining straps were also scarlet (see Plate 7).

At first there was no distinction between sapeurs 2nd and 3rd class, both wearing the shako. With the forming of the Young Guard companies, the sapeurs 2nd class of the Old Guard wore the helmet. With the sapeurs 1st class, however, a distinctive marking was used. This appeared as corporals stripes on the left arm only and were two angled aurore wool

Fig 37

ABOVE: A: Sapeur in full dress with black winter gaiters. B: Sapeur in full dress with white summer gaiters. C: Sapeur in tenue de marche in greatcoat. The roll on the pack is a grey blanket. This was folded inside the blue greatcoat when that was carried rolled on the pack. D: Sapeur Genie officer in surtout. E: Sapeur of the Young Guard. F: Sapeur, 1815. Note the shaped black short gaiters with black leather buttons.

bars piped scarlet. Corporals wore the stripes above both cuffs. Fourriers (quartermasters) wore corporals stripes plus a gold angled stripe on each upper sleeve.

Sergeants and sergeant majors wore one or two gold stripes, piped scarlet, above each cuff. The epaulettes of the fourrier and sergeant had the strap edged with gold lace, gold retaining straps and half moons and mixed red and gold fringes.

Sergeant majors wore the same but with gold fringes. The grenades on the turnbacks were of gold for the fourrier and NCOs and the sword knot tassel was mixed red and gold. Service stripes were red for men and corporals, gold for fourriers and NCOs.

Officers wore identical coats to the men but of better quality. The standard gold epaulettes on the left and contra-epaulette and aiguilette on the right was used to define rank. Buttons were gilt and turnback grenades gold.

For service wear the officers wore, in conjunction with the chapeau previously mentioned, a surtout. This had a black velvet collar and black velvet round cuffs, both piped scarlet. The turnbacks were also scarlet with gold grenades. Normal rank markings were worn (see Fig 37D).

In working dress the men wore a long sleeved blue waistcoat which was also worn under the habit coat, and long blue trousers, usually rolled up a little at the bottoms. The bonnet de police completed this style of dress which was called tenue de travail. As mentioned above all ranks wore the blue waistcoat under the habit coat.

For full dress wear, blue breeches were worn with long black gaiters in winter and long white gaiters in summer. The black gaiters had brass buttons and the white gaiters white cloth covered buttons. For tenue de route, grey gaiters were worn and these usually had leather buttons. These were normally worn under the blue trousers.

The sapeurs who acted as conductors (drivers) wore light cream coloured skin breeches and long riding boots with knee guards. The officers were all mounted and wore long riding boots. The greatcoats were dark blue with two rows of brass buttons down the front. The equipment

BELOW AND OPPOSITE PAGE: Fire pump used by the Sapeurs du Genie. This was drawn by two horses harnessed as for the artillery caisson. The water reservoir illustrated below was protected by a faun coloured canvas cover.

Fig 38

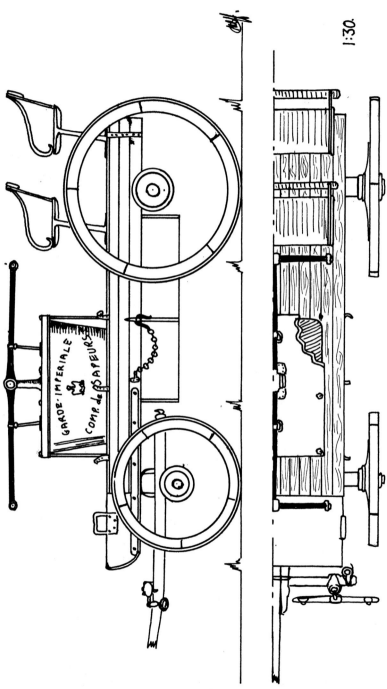

1:30.

GARDE·IMPERIALE
COMP. de SAPEURS

of the sapeurs was identical to that of the Grenadiers à pied with only minor variations. The muskets for instance had white metal strappings and the bayonet scabbard appears to have been made of black leather. The pouch flap was decorated with only a brass eagle, no grenades, and in tenue de route a white cloth cover was placed over the pouch flap upon which a black crowned eagle was painted.

The horse furniture of the men who were drivers consisted of a half sheepskin, edged with scarlet vandyking, worn over a brown leather French saddle.

Officers had a blue saddle cloth with either a blue covered or a white leather saddle. The edge of the saddle cloth had a gold lace stripe as had the double tiered pistol hoods. A gold crown was set at an angle in the rear corners. The layouts of one of the Sapeurs' fire pumps is shown in Fig 38. This was painted dark green with the water reservoir of copper. The inscription shown on the reservoir was in gold. The sapeurs also had caissons, wagons and probably forges. The four horse team for the pump was harnessed in the same way as to a limber and gun. For fuller details see *French Napoleonic Artillery*.

BELOW: A sapeur in tenue de sortie in greatcoat, with two Grenadiers on tenue de sortie. Note the seated figure has the bearskin in place of the bicorne. (Collection of Colonel Druene).

The Regiments of Tirailleurs

The Tirailleurs were first formed from the regiments of Tirailleurs Grenadiers and Conscrits Grenadiers, and wore an almost identical uniform to the Tirailleurs Grenadiers. Consequently we will note here the differences involved and refer the reader to the section concerned with the Tirailleurs Grenadiers for further information.

The shako was identical but for scarlet cords and plume and at first the regiments, up to the 6th, were distinguished as follows:

1st Regiment   Red over white pom-pon
2nd Regiment   White over white pom-pon
3rd Regiment   Red lentile disc with white centre
4th Regiment   Either white lentile disc with red centre or all red
5th Regiment   Either white lentile disc with blue centre or all white
6th Regiment   Blue lentile disc with white centre

After April 1813 all regiments wore a red plume for full dress or a red pom-pon for service dress.

The remainder of the uniform was identical to the Tirailleurs Grenadiers.

During the '100 Days' the habit veste was worn. These had red collars without piping. The red turnbacks were ornamented with white eagles. The pockets were piped white as were the lapels. The pointed cuffs were scarlet piped white and red epaulettes were worn. The white chevrons were not carried on the shakos and only a red pom-pon was worn. No cords or plume appears to have been worn. White breeches and short black gaiters completed the attire plus the usual equipment except that the sabre briquet only appears to have been used by NCOs. Consequently only the pouch belt was worn and the bayonets affixed at the front of this (see Fig 39A and Plate 6).

Voltigeurs

Following the same pattern as the Tirailleurs, the Voltigeurs of the Guard were formed from the regiments of Tirailleurs Chasseurs and Conscrits Chasseurs. The uniform was almost identical to the Tirailleurs Chasseurs and again the reader should refer back to the appropriate section for further details. It is probable that the plume of the Voltigeurs was red over green in equal proportions with either a yellow or green pom-pon, which was worn without the plume for service wear.

The collar of the coat was either yellow or buff in colour, piped blue.

Green epaulettes were worn with yellow half moons. It is possible that the green eagles and horns on the turnbacks were replaced by eagles in some cases.

As with the Tirailleurs, the '100 Days' saw the Voltigeurs in the 1812 style habit veste, identical to that described for the Tirailleurs except for a green pom-pon on the shako.

Yellow collars and green epaulettes with yellow half moons on the coats and green eagles on the turnbacks. Equipment was as before with the same exception regarding the sabre briquet as noted for the Tirailleurs of this period (see Fig 39B and Plates 5 and 6).

Fig 39

ABOVE: A: Tirailleur, 1815. B: Voltigeur Sergeant, 1815. C: Tirailleur Officer, 1815.

Pupilles de la Garde

While forming part of the Dutch army the regiment had worn white coats with different coloured facings for each company. As part of the Imperial Guard the following uniform was specified (see Fig 39 D and E and Plate 6). A Green habit veste with the collar, lapels, pointed cuffs, shoulder straps and turnbacks piped yellow. Yellow wool eagles appeared on the turnbacks. The breeches were white and calf length black gaiters were worn. The shako was black with white lace chevrons at each side. The cords and flounders were green. At the front of the shako a brass eagle plate was worn and above the cockade a round yellow pom-pon was carried. The chin scales were of brass. The greatcoat was a beige fawn colour and the field service cap was green, piped and tasselled yellow. A single whitened leather cross belt was worn over the left shoulder to support the cartridge pouch which had a small brass crowned eagle on its flap.

The bayonet scabbard was attached to the front of this belt. The sabre briquet was not carried by the Pupilles but it is possible that NCOs may have worn them, in which case, of course, the two crossbelts would appear. A dragoon pattern musket, shorter than the normal infantry musket, was carried by the Pupilles who were after all no older than 19 and as young as 14.

Corporals were distinguished by two inverted yellow chevrons above each cuff. Sergeants and sergeant majors were distinguished by one or two gold lace inverted chevrons above each cuff. It is possible that NCOs may have worn epaulettes with green straps edged gold, gold half moons and mixed green and gold fringes. Their turnback eagles may also have been gold and the shako cords mixed green and gold.

The officers wore a similar uniform to the men but the chevrons on the sides of the shako were silver and senior officers had a gold lace top band. The cords and flounders were gold and the plume yellow. A white plume was worn by senior officers. The normal rank indications were shown by means of silver and gold contra epaulettes. The gorget plate was gilt. Foot officers wore turned down knee boots and mounted officers high riding boots. The officers carried a light sword with a gilt hilt and a gold lace sword knot.

The sword in wear was suspended from a white leather waist belt. Mounted officers had a green square horse cloth and a white leather French saddle. The saddle cloth was edged with a gold lace stripe and in the rear corners appeared a gold eagle. Three tiered holster covers were carried at the front of the saddle and were of green cloth edged with gold lace. This then was the regulation dress prescribed in the decree of May 1811. In December of the same year another decree ordered that the 1st, 2nd, 3rd and 4th battalions and the first two companies of the Depot company only should be dressed in green. The 5th, 6th and 7th battalions and the 3rd and 4th companies of the Depot battalion were to wear white uniforms of the same style as the green ones. The piping and the decorations on the white uniforms were to be crimson. All battalions were to wear the same style shako, beige overcoat and brass eagle buttons.

It is, however, very doubtful if either of these regulations were implemented very quickly and it is probable that the Pupilles continued to wear the white uniforms with different coloured facings that were worn in Dutch service until they wore out. A report on a review in 1812 furnishes us with the following information on the uniforms of the 1st battalion. General Deriot reports that the 1st company wore white coatees with

---

BELOW: D: Pupille in Dutch style uniform. E: Pupille in regulation dress. F: Flanqueur Chasseur.

Fig 39

D   E   F

crimson collar, lapels and cuffs, the 2nd company wore white coatees with lapels and collars in most cases green, in others sky blue and yellow. The 3rd company wore white coatees with most collars and lapels sky blue but others yellow and pink, the 4th company wore white coatees with green collars and lapels.

Where the battalion or company wore a white coat, then there too the officers wore white coats. It is possible that the Tête du Colonnes were all dressed in green to avoid a mix up when parading together. In any case only the green version of their uniform is known and this is given in Section 4.

Flanqueur Grenadiers

In their short existance the Flanqueur Grenadiers wore a shako identical to that of the Fusilier Grenadiers but with red cords and flounders and a red over yellow spherical pom-pon (see Plate 6).

The 1812 style coatee was worn made of green cloth. The collar, lapels and pointed shoulder straps were green, piped yellow, as were the vertical pockets.

The pointed cuffs and the turnbacks were scarlet, piped yellow and white cloth eagles were worn on the turnbacks.

White breeches with short black gaiters were worn. These sometimes took the form of heart shaped gaiters with yellow braiding at the tops and yellow tassels in the 'V'.

The equipment was exactly as described for the Pupilles but with steel grey greatcoats. Rank distinctions also followed the Pupilles but as little documentation exists it has not been possible to find exact reference to the rank distinctions. It is probable, however that NCOs had gold lace edged epaulette straps of green with gold half moons and mixed red and gold fringes. Continuing this logical deduction we can also suggest the shako cords were mixed red and gold and that the shako chevrons were scarlet edged with gold piping. The turnback eagles would also be gold and a sabre briquet would be carried. Sword knots would probably be mixed red and gold. Regarding the dress of the officers we suggest the same distinctions as proposed for the officers of the Pupilles.

Flanqueur Chasseurs

The uniform worn was identical to that of the Flanqueur Grenadiers but with green cuffs. On the turnbacks green horns appeared in place of white eagles. The shako did not have white chevrons and the cords and flounders were white instead of red. A carrot shaped pom-pon of yellow over green in equal proportions was worn. Where heart topped gaiters were worn the braiding and tassels were green (see Plate 6).

NCOs distinctions would probably be as suggested for the Flanqueur Grenadiers but with green in place of red. However, shako cords would probably be mixed white and gold.

Officers were as for the Pupilles but with shakos the same as officers of the Fusiliers Chasseurs. Equipment as for the Pupilles.

4: Uniforms of the Têtes du Colonnes

IN this section we will be describing the uniforms of the 'Têtes du Colonnes' or heads of columns, which consisted of the drum major, sapeurs, drummers and musicians. The Grenadiers will be covered in great detail showing the changes of uniform detail and the various styles over the years. The other regiments must, perforce, be given a less detailed coverage and in certain instances it has been impossible to unearth details of the dress of the drum majors and musicians.

As, in most cases, the basic uniform style was similar to the regimental uniform we will not follow the same style as in Section 3 but concentrate on the differences and describe the variations, etc, as they arise. Reference to Sections 2 and 3 will clarify any additional points. Where possible we will cover the drum major first, followed by the sapeurs, drummers and finally the musicians.

Grenadiers à Pied

The drum major wore a bicorne with the edge laced gold and with gold stiffeners, cockade strap and tassels. During the Consulate period the plume was coloured scarlet at the top, then white, then blue. At this time a tri-coloured feather edging is also shown on the chapeau of the drum major.

After 1805 a cluster of three feathers at the base of a white 'panache' plume was worn for full dress. The feathers, viewed from the front, were coloured crimson, white and sky blue (see Plate 9H).

The standard style habit coat was worn with the addition of gold lace with a scalloped edge, to the collar, lapels, cuffs and turnbacks. Until 1805, the scarlet cuffs carried three rings of gold lace around them, including the lace edging. This was discontinued after 1805 and plain scarlet cuffs edged with a single lace appeared. This gold lacing also appeared around the seams of the armhole, the seams and rear of the sleeves, and the rear seams (see Plate 9A and B).

The vertical pockets were laced gold and piped scarlet at the edge. A gold lace 'taile' was worn around the rear waist buttons. Between 1804-05 the button holes on the lapels, pockets and side buttons were laced gold and buttons were gilt.

This particular lacing does not appear after 1805 in the majority of contemporary prints, so one assumes it was discontinued. The white waistcoat was laced with gold as was the white leather waist belt (the waist belt plate was gold with an embossed grenade).

The breeches were white with gold scalloped lacing on the outside seams and ornate gold Hungarian knots at the front. Some prints show gold lace passing down the front of the breeches into the crutch. The 'grande tenue' in 1802 shows distinctive spearhead designs as shown in Fig 41A.

The white cuff flaps were edged with gold lace until 1805 and after appear with only a narrow gold edging or even plain white. Above the cuffs were two gold lace stripes as already described for NCOs and the epaulettes were all gold. Gold grenades were carried on the scarlet turnbacks.

Gauntlet gloves were worn on parade with light ochre gloves and white leather gauntlets. The white gauntlet part being laced with gold. The belt, worn over the right shoulder, was scarlet with gold lace fringes, and ornaments.

The plate on the belt was gilt with miniature ebony drum sticks. This was a relic of the days when the drum major was the senior drummer and also carried a drum. The sword was carried from the waist belt in a black leather scabbard with a gilt heel and hilt. The sword knot and tassel were gold.

Until 1805, the short Hussar style boots were laced around the tops and down the fronts as shown in Fig 41A. Note the gold fringe and the front of the boot forming a point instead of the more usual 'V'. Sometime after 1805 the more usual boots appeared which were not as ornate as the first style worn being the Hussar style with gold lace around the tops and a gold tassel hanging from the 'V'. By the end of the Empire, certain contemporary prints show the full dress uniform to be in fact identical to the 'petite tenue' or service dress (undress), it is probable that this would have been the style of dress worn at the Waterloo period.

For the 'petit tenue' the normal Grenadier habit coat or the surtout was worn with the addition of two lines of gold lace on the collar and cuffs. The rank stripes and gold epaulettes were the same as already described for full dress. The bicorne was plain with only the stiffeners, tassels and cockade strap in gilt. A scarlet plume was worn. The waistcoat and breeches were plain white and turned down boots were worn. In some instances the boots were not turned down but reached to the knee. The epée was carried on a plain white leather waist belt which had a gilt plate bearing an embossed grenade (see Fig 41C). For winter wear blue trousers were worn over the boots or tucked inside the boots. Also a double breasted 'redingcote' was worn, which was plain blue with gilt buttons, and carried the rank stripes and epaulettes. A Hussar style belt with an 'S' clasp was normally worn with this coat.

The drum major on the campaign of 1814 is shown wearing petite tenue with the habit coat and wearing the scarlet and gold belt. His trousers are blue with a gold lace stripe down the outside seams; see Fig 41D.

At the time of Waterloo the drum major is shown wearing the same uniform as above but with white breeches and boots turned up to the knee. No shoulder belt was worn in this instance.

In tenue de ville the petite tenue would be born with white breeches and white stockings. Black shoes with silver buckles would be worn

Fig 40

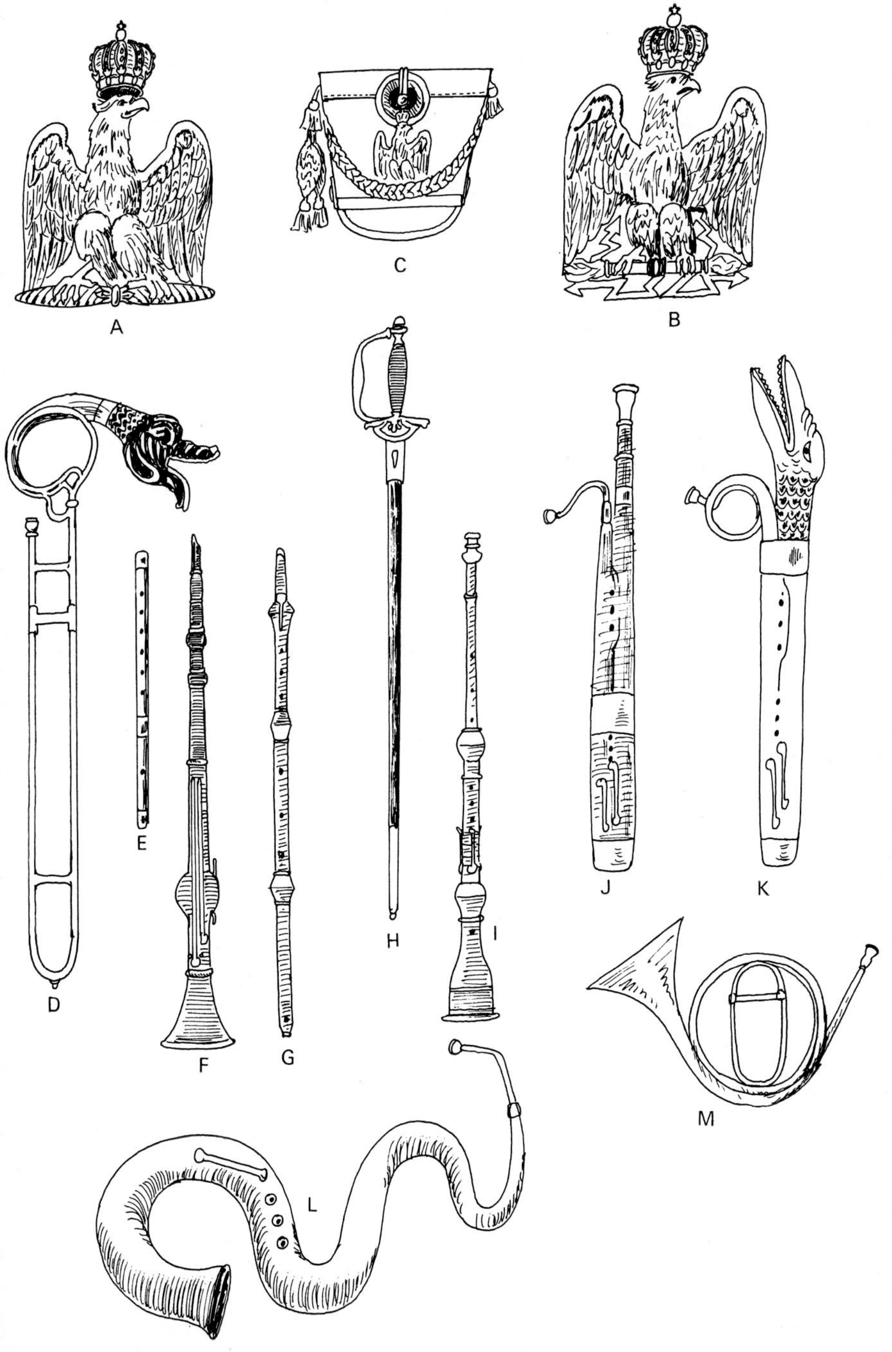

A   B   C   D   E   F   G   H   I   J   K   L   M

77

and a silver headed cane carried. The epée would usually be carried on the waist belt which passed through the front flap of the breeches; see Fig 41E.

Tenue de sortie (walking out dress) was usually the surtout, white or fawn breeches and boots 'a la Souvarov'; see Fig 41F.

The drum major's staff was carried on most occasions when leading the band (but not in tenue de ville or tenue de sortie). This was of natural wood, with the top and ferrule at the bottom in gilt. The cords and tassels were gold.

Tambour Maitre (Drum master)

Each battalion furnished a tambour maitre or drum master who would deputize for the drum major as the need arose. There were in fact two drum masters in 1799, three in 1800, two in 1801 and three again in 1804. When the 2nd Regiment was formed there were six but one became the drum major of the new regiment (see Plate 9C and Fig 42A).

The uniform was the standard Grenadier habit coat with gold lace on the collar, lapels, cuffs and turnbacks. The sleeve seams were also laced gold, front and rear while the cuff flaps were edged with a narrower gold lace. The button holes were edged with gold lace on the lapels and pockets, and all buttons were yellow brass. The gold lace 'taille' appeared on the rear waist buttons. The pockets were outlined with gold lace and piped scarlet at the edges. Breeches followed the pattern worn by the Grenadiers. The hat had gold lace edging and gold stiffeners, cockade strap and tassels. A scarlet plume was worn. It is important to note that while the drum major normally wore his hat 'en bataille', ie, in line with the shoulders, the drum master wore his 'fore and aft', 'en colonne'. The epaulettes, rank and service stripes were identical to those already described for the sergeant. The standard sabre briquet was carried on a white shoulder belt with stitched edges and a brass grenade was attached to it on the chest. Yellow ochre wrist gloves were worn and the standard shoulder pack and rolled greatcoat was carried on the march, etc. The drum master carried a staff or mace similar to that of the drum major but had a silver head and ferrule, and red cords and tassels.

The style of dress worn for tenue de ville, tenue de route, etc, followed that already described for the Grenadier NCOs.

Sapeurs

The sapeurs of the Grenadiers á pied wore many variations of the standard uniform and it is an almost impossible task to describe them all. In particular the decorations on the crossed belts prove very difficult to describe in correct chronological order and therefore the reader must accept a degree of uncertainty although all descriptions are based on reliable or contemporary sources (see Plate 9 D and E).

OPPOSITE PAGE: A: Drum Major, full dress, 1802. B: Drum Major, full dress, 1810. C: Drum Major in petit tenue or service dress. D: Drum Major in campaign dress, 1814. Note the sash is without fringes. E: Drum Major in tenue de ville. F: Drum Major in tenue de sortie wearing surtout.

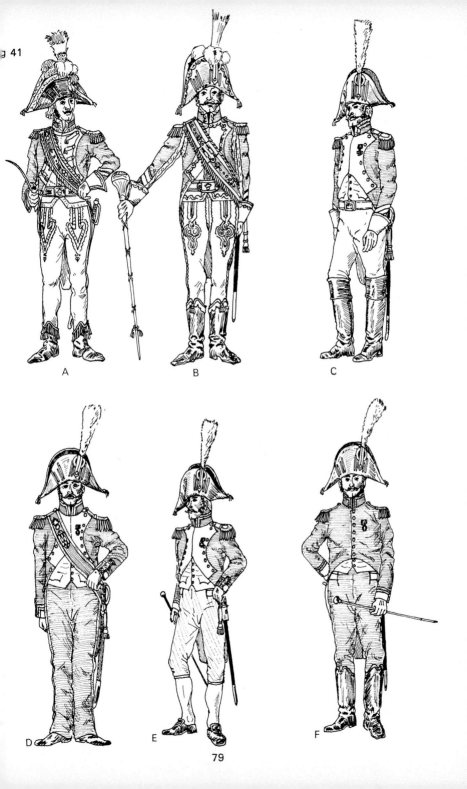

A   B   C

D   E   F

Before 1800 the Consular Guard had no sapeurs but in September of that year they were raised with two sapeurs to each company. As the regiment consisted of two battalions, each of eight companies, there were 32 sapeurs plus a sergeant sapeur and a corporal sapeur. In 1806 the regiment only had four companies per battalion so that the sapeur strength was reduced to 16 plus the sergeant and corporal.

In 1800 the uniform of the sapeur was the same as that of the Grenadier of the period with the epaulettes of the Grenadiers. The bearskin was without a plate and had white cords. The bonnet patch was scarlet with an aurore lace cross. On the upper arms, red crossed axes on a white outline were worn. The decoration on the belts probably consisted of grenades over crossed axes in brass. It is possible that cords of mixed red and gold were worn and the axes on the arms were gold and red.

By 1803 the dress followed that of sergeants of the Grenadiers with mixed red and gold cords and a gold lace cross on the scarlet bonnet patch (in 1808 following the regimental pattern, the cross was replaced by a gold grenade). The epaulettes were scarlet with gold lace edging to the straps and gold crescents. For full dress the axes on the arms were gold edged red and for use on the surtout (service dress) they were of red cloth edged gold (see Plate 9L). The turnback ornaments were crossed axes. Gold for full dress, red edged gold for service dress.

Probably in 1806, the epaulettes were the same as for a sergeant of the Grenadiers, ie, the fringe was gold over scarlet.

Apart from this and various details on the belts which we will consider later, the uniform remained unchanged until 1810 when the sapeurs received an elaborate new uniform for full dress wear. The new dress was basically the same as already described but with the addition of mixed red and gold lace, 22 mm wide, on the collar, lapels, turnbacks and sleeve seams. The pocket flaps were also outlined with this lace and edged with scarlet piping. The cuffs were edged with mixed red and gold lace, 13 mm wide. The narrower lace also outlined the button holes of the lapels and pockets, ending in mixed red and gold fringes. The crossed axes on the upper arms of this coat were gold, edged red. In some instances gold grenades, edged red are shown above the axes and even in some cases below also. The turnbacks were decorated with gold crossed axes (see Plate 9E). At this time a 'second' coat, issued for service wear was introduced. This was identical to the Grenadier coat but with gold lace on the collar, cuffs and turnbacks. The arm axes badge was of red cloth edged gold. Prior to this date the service dress had been the surtout, identical to that worn by the Grenadiers with axes, red edged gold on the arms and turnbacks. This coat was retained in 1810 as 'petit tenue' for walking out and had the addition of gold lace to the collar and cuffs.

OPPOSITE PAGE: A: Tambour Maitre. B: Sapeur, 1802. C: Sapeur, 1808-9. D: Sapeur, tenue de marche, in greatcoat, 1809. E: Sapeur, tenue de ville. F: Sapeur, grande tenue, 1810-14.

Fig 42

A   B   C

D   E   F

This tenue de sortie or walking out dress consisted of a chapeau with stiffeners, cockade strap and tassels of mixed scarlet and gold, and a scarlet carrot shaped pom-pon. The surtout was as described and a white waistcoat was worn. The breeches were either fawn or white and either white stockings and black buckle shoes or boots 'a la Souvarov' were worn. As this dress was worn from 1805 the epaulettes were at first scarlet with gold crescents and gold edging to the straps and later as the epaulettes of sergeants (see Fig 42C).

Fig 42D, shows a sapeur in tenue de route, circa 1809. Note the wearing of the bicorne with the bearskin rolled in its bag. Also the apron worn over the greatcoat. All buttons were yellow brass. With all the styles of dress, except petit tenue, a buff leather apron was worn, usually with the top under the coat or surtout. The outer face of the apron was whitened.

The distinctive feature of the sapeurs was, of course, the full beard, always dark, and the hair was powered and tied with a black ribbon.

The equipment of the sapeurs consisted of the normal sabre belt, although the sabre was of a different pattern, a belt 'porte hache' which carried the axe, the axe itself and a short musket. The pack and greatcoat were as for the Grenadiers. Note, however, the crossed axes, red edged gold and the epaulettes were worn on the greatcoat.

Firstly the sabres carried by the Sapeurs differed from those of the ordinary Grenadier by having at first a straight blade; later curved versions were used. One edge, as shown, was serrated. The main distinctions, however, was in the hilt which was brass and topped, under the Consuls, by the head of a cock. Under the Empire this was gradually replaced by the head of an eagle (see Figs 43A, D and E). The scabbard was of black leather with brass heel and top. This style of sabre was extremely heavy and on campaign was usually replaced by the standard sabre briquet with the sword knot of the troop. The axe had a blackened wood shaft with a brass ferrule and a steel head. The 'porte hache' was carried on a whitened leather belt which fastened by a brass buckle and slide. The end was bound with brass. The decoration of the belt appears to have varied immensely and consisted of brass grenades, crossed axes and tetes de medusa (see Fig 43C). The following are some combinations noted: Crossed axes on both belts below point of crossing. Grenades on both belts below point of crossing with crossed axes beneath grenade on sabre belt (Consular Guard). The 'porte hache' itself was usually of black leather and fastened by three straps and brass buckles. The shaft of the axe rested upon the back and was held in place by a loop on the belt.

At first the small cartridge case was not carried on the 'porte hache' but was adopted in 1802-3 by the Chasseurs so it is likely that it was at this time it made its appearance with the Grenadiers.

Prior to this a small cartridge pouch was carried on the waist belt at the front. The uniform worn on campaign in 1806-7 (see Fig 44A), consisting of the surtout, also shows a cartridge box on the waist belt at the front. In this case the eagle and grenade appear. As the musket does not appear to have been carried before 1805, this pouch probably carried cartridges for the pistol which was carried on the waist belt. Around 1806 a brass eagle appeared on the cartridge pouch of

Fig 43

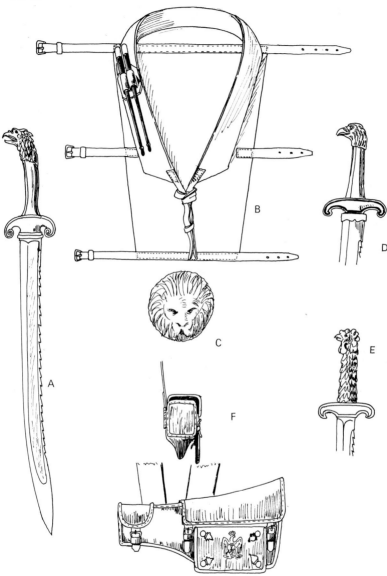

ABOVE: A: Sapeur's sabre. B: Drum apron and carriage. C: Tete de medusa ornament. D and E: Variations on sapeur's sabre hilts. 'E' represents a cock's head which was probably used under the Consuls. F: Detail of 'Porte-Hache'.

the 'porte hache', later the small grenades in the corners followed (see Fig 43F). The musket was of the Dragoon type shorter than the standard musket.

On parade the sapeur carried the axe on the right shoulder, held by the right hand with the blade facing to the front. The musket was slung on the left shoulder with the bayonet fixed. The sergeant sapeurs did not carry an axe, and therefore had, no 'porte hache' but a normal pouch. He paraded with sabre held in the right hand and musket slung on left shoulder with fixed bayonet.

Drummers (Tambours)

The strength of the drummers was the same as the sapeurs, that is two per company. The full dress uniform varied little during the period of the Empire. Basically the same habit coat of the Grenadiers was worn with the addition of mixed gold and scarlet lace on the lapels, pockets and coat front edges (see Plate 9F). Around 1805 the mixed gold and scarlet lacing appeared on the turnbacks also. The button holes were laced with brandenbergs ending in tassels, all in mixed gold and scarlet. The vertical pockets were piped on the edges with scarlet. The inverted 'W' lacing or 'taille' on the rear waist buttons was also mixed gold and scarlet. The collar, cuffs and cuff flaps were laced gold. Under the epaulettes appeared 'nids de hirondelles' or swallows nests. They were scarlet, edged with gold lace. In 1808 these disappeared and it is probable that it was at this time that the lacing which had previously been gold became mixed gold and scarlet (see Plate 9G). The turnbacks were ornamented by gold grenades which at least around 1805 were on white cloth patches. Later the patches did not appear. Buttons were yellow brass. The bearskin of the drummer was identical to that worn by the Grenadier with white cords. The sabre briquet was also identical to that carried by the Grenadiers, while the epaulettes were the same as for sergeants, though these changed in appearance in 1806.

In tenue de route or on campaign the drummers wore the same uniforms as the Grenadiers (see Fig 44 D and E). That is the surtout until 1809 and the 'second' habit coat or petit tenue after. Both garments had the collar and cuffs laced gold. Some prints show the surtout with pointed cuffs laced gold, but the round version is more likely. The cuffs of the 'second' coat were laced gold and the flaps were also laced gold but much narrower.

The surtout and 'second' coat were normally seen with plain scarlet Grenadiers' epaulettes. For tenue de ville either the surtout or full dress coat appears to have been worn with full dress epaulettes and either white stockings and buckle shoes (summer) or boots 'a la Souvarov' (winter). The sabre briquet was carried on the shoulder belt. In all examples of dress the waistcoat and legwear followed the pattern for the Grenadiers.

The greatcoat was identical to that of the Grenadiers. The 'collier porte-caisse' or drum belt was of whitened leather with a brass 'porte baquette' or drum stick holder on the chest. Above this a brass grenade appeared. Both these items were sometimes mounted on a scarlet patch (Fig 43B).

The drum is shown as having stamped brass grenades on the drum

ABOVE: A: Sapeur, tenue de campagne, 1806-7. B: Drummer, full dress, 1804-5. C: Drummer, tenue de ville in full dress coat. D: Drummer, tenue de campagne, 1810-14. E: Drummer, tenue de campagne, 1806-7. F: Negro cymbals player.

between tensioner cords, but it is impossible to say when these appeared. The rims are also subject to a degree of uncertainty (see Plate 9M).

At the time of the end of the Consulate the rims were light blue divided into lozenges by white lines, in each lozenge was painted a yellow grenade. Around 1807 the rims are shown painted in triangles. Those with their bases at the outer edge were white while those with their bases inside were alternatively red and mid blue. Later the rims were light to mid blue with painted yellow grenades between the white tensioner ropes. At the base of the drum, two whitened leather carrying straps were attached to the encircling rope around the bottom rim. The drum was hooked on to a leather loop attached to a ring on the drum carriage.

Musicians

The band of the Grenadiers à pied varied in number over the years. In 1799 there were 25 musicians and a bandmaster, 50 musicians and two band masters in 1800, 46 in 1804 and 40 in 1806. It is probable that further reductions took place later but it is not possible to confirm this. Anyone intent on modelling the band of the Grenadiers must arrive at his own conclusions as to the number of bandsmen and the arrangement of the instruments. A theoretical layout is shown in Appendix 4, but this is based on general information and is not documented as the exact arrangement of the Grenadiers.

BELOW: A: Musician, 1802-3. Note only five buttons on each lapel. B: Musician, 1810-11. C: Musician, petit tenue or tenue de ville, 1810-14.

Fig 45

A   B   C

From the time of the Consulate, the uniforms of the musicians consisted of blue coat with crimson facings. Under the Consuls a habit coat like that of the Grenadier was worn with a crimson collar, lapels and round crimson cuffs. The turnbacks were also crimson with gold grenades. The collar, lapels, cuffs, turnbacks and pockets were edged with gold lace. It is of interest to note that the drum major and the musicians under the Consulate had only five buttons on the lapels (see Plate 9A and Fig 45A). The button holes on the lapels and on the pockets were edged with gold lace and gold tassels as were the three buttons and button holes on either side of the coat. The 'taille' at the rear waist was also of gold lace. The chapeau was edged with gold lace and the stiffeners, cockade strap and tassel were gold. A mixed crimson and white feathered edging appeared on the chapeau and a crimson or a crimson, white, crimson (in equal parts) plume was worn (see Plate 9I).

An epée was carried on a whitened leather waist belt with a gilt plate bearing a grenade. This was worn over the waistcoat at first but from 1810, at least, was usually worn under the flap at the front of the breeches. The hilt of the epée was gilt with a gold sword knot (see Fig 40H). The scabbard was of black leather with a gilt heel. Until 1810, white gaiters were worn on parade but after that date turned down boots were worn. Before this date the boots were worn for service or ordinary wear (see Fig 45 B and C).

Under the Empire, from 1804, the lapels had the normal seven buttons and the cuffs had a white cuff flap, edged gold.

The hat was also modified under the Empire and a 'panache' or cluster of ostrich feathers was worn, crimson, white and crimson. The plume which rose from the centre of the feathers was white. As with the Grenadiers the surtout and the 'second' coat were worn for service and tenue de ville. These were identical to those worn by the Grenadiers but with the addition of gold lace on the collar and cuffs of the surtout and gold lace on the collar, cuffs and cuff flaps of the coat. The passants or epaulettes strap were gold as were the grenades on the turnbacks. In some instances the pocket of the surtout were piped crimson instead of the Grenadiers' scarlet. Fawn leather gloves were worn.

For tenue de ville the chapeaux were minus the lacing and feathered edge, but the stiffeners, cockade strap and tassels were gold. A scarlet plume was worn. The waistcoat and breeches were usually white in all styles of dress but in tenue de ville either white stockings and buckle shoes or boots 'a la Souvarov' were worn. Blue breeches were sometimes worn in tenue ordinaire or de ville in winter (see Fig 41F).

According to one source, Marco de Saint Hilaire, the dress of the musicians was changed in 1810 but the other sources do not confirm this. For the reader's interest the information is included but the author personally is not convinced that the change took place. Basically the crimson facings gave way to facings of scarlet and boots 'a la Souvarov' were worn in full dress. The hat was without stiffeners, lace or feathered edge and a white over scarlet plume was worn (see Plate 9N).

It is probable, however, that from around 1811, the brandenbergs or lacing to the button holes were discontinued. In all styles of dress, gold 'trefoil' shoulder straps were worn lined crimson (scarlet if Saint Hilaire is to be believed).

Finally Fig 44F, shows a negro cymbalier attributed to the band of the Grenadiers à pied in 1802. The head-dress was crimson with a light green turban and white plume over yellow. Decorations and fringes were gold. Coat was blue with a crimson collar and turnbacks. All lacing was gold. It is not possible to be precise on the cuffs as they were hidden by gauntlet gloves which were light green. They were probably round, crimson in colour and laced gold. Above the cuffs were three spaced gold lace inverted chevrons. The waistcoat and breeches were crimson, braided and decorated with gold lace. The waist belt was white with a gilt plate and supported a standard epée. The epaulettes were also gold. The short boots were black with gold tassels and lacing.

Before proceeding with the remaining regiments the author would point out that the same detail cannot be given to all the other drummers, musicians, etc, but sufficient information can be given to enable the collector or historian to recognise the basic uniforms worn.

Grenadiers Hollandais

As has already been described the Grenadiers Hollandais were formally part of the Dutch Royal Guard, and the Têtes du Colonne retained their former Dutch uniforms. The uniforms of the Dutch Grenadiers is very well documented with regard to the Têtes du Colonne. In fact, so much evidence is contradictory that it is not possible to formulate the dates which these uniforms were worn. The material is therefore placed before the reader as it has been found. It can be stated with some degree of certainty that in 1810 there were 30 drummers, 20 fifers and 14 musicians in the band. The fifers were aged between 14 and 19, and the youngest was only 4 feet 2½ inches tall. These uniforms appear to have been identical with the drummers but without, of course, the drum and carriage.

Drum Major

The drum major wore the 1810-11 chapeau, 'en bataille' (across the shoulders) with scalloped gold lace on the edge, stiffeners, cockade strap and tassel pulls were also gold. A feathered edge to the chapeau was coloured red, white and blue. A 'panache' of ostrich feathers, sky blue, white and scarlet was carried and from the centre rose a white plume (see Plate 10B). The long tailed coat had square lapels and cuffs. The coat itself was 'bleu ciel fonce': deep sky blue with a yellow collar, lapels, cuffs, cuff flaps and turnbacks. All these items were edged with gold lace except for the cuff flaps. The turnbacks carried gold grenade ornaments. The shoulder and sleeve seams were also decorated with gold lace. All the button holes had gold lace brandenbergs with tassels and the buttons at the rear waist (taille) had an inverted 'W' of gold lace. Two angled gold lace stripes were worn on each sleeve above the cuffs and on the left arm two inverted chevrons of gold lace were worn (service stripes, See Plate 10A).

Gold epaulettes were worn and buttons were gilt. The drum majors shoulder belt was white, edged with gold lace and decorated with gold oak leaves. A gilt 'baguette' holder carried miniature drum sticks. In this case the belt supported the sabre which had a stylized eagles head and a black leather scabbard richly ornamented with gilt as shown in

Plate 10D. The white waistcoat was edged with gold lace as were the waistcoat pocket flaps. The white breeches had ornate Hungarian knots and stripes on the outside seams of gold lace. Hussar style boots were worn with gold lace edging and tassels. Gauntlet gloves were worn in white with gold lace edging to the cuffs. The drum majors baton was of natural wood with a silver head and ferrule. The baton cords were gold (see Fig 46A).

In 1811 as near as can be ascertained the chapeau was replaced by a black fur colpack or Hussar busby. This had gold cords and flounders, a deep yellow 'bag', laced gold and the same 'panache' and plume as on the chapeau (see Plate 10C). Another source (Fallou) gives an almost identical uniform but with the lace and brandenbergs in silver. In fact by substituting silver where gold appears in the foregoing description we have the uniform described by Fallou. In addition the cuff flaps were white, edged silver and the shoulder belt was scarlet with silver decorations and fringes. Only the colpack is cited in this instance with a yellow bag, piped silver with a silver tassel, and a panache of white feathers and a sky blue plume with a white tip.

The Alsace Collection gives details for the drum major as follows. Crimson habit coat with square lapels. The collar, lapels, cuffs and turnbacks are white. There is a gold lace edging to the collar, lapels and cuffs. The buttons are gilt with gold lace brandenbergs on the button holes of the lapels and pockets, which were also edged with gold lace. Gold trefoil shoulder straps were worn and on each cuff there were two gold lace angled stripes. On the left upper arm were two gold lace inverted chevrons. The waistcoat and breeches were identical to those already described. The bicorne was worn with gold lace to the edge and a gold lace cockade strap. Above the cockade was a panache of blue feathers and a scarlet plume. The shoulder belt was black with gold braid and gold decorations. Turned down boots were worn. The mace had a silver head and silver cords. The last description is as follows: The habit coat was sky blue with crimson collar, square lapels, cuffs and turnbacks. The collar, lapels and cuffs were edged with silver lace. A plain white waistcoat and white breeches were worn with turned down boots. Silver epaulettes were worn on the shoulders and the buttons were also silver. The shoulder belt was crimson with silver decorations. A black colpack was worn with a crimson bag, piped and tasseled silver, silver cords, a panache of white feathers with a sky blue plume tipped white.

Sapeurs

The generally accepted dress for the sapeur of the Grenadiers Hollandais was identical to the normal dress of the Grenadiers with the addition of mixed gold and crimson lace to the collar, lapels, cuffs, cuff flaps, turnbacks and inside the crimson piping of the pockets. Gold crossed axes on a scarlet patch appeared on each arm. The bearskin had mixed crimson and gold cords and flounders with a scarlet plume (see Fig 46C). All other details followed the styles used by the Grenadiers Francais, ie, epaulettes of a sergeant. Again we find a completely different description in the Carl Collection which attributes to the sapeurs of the Grenadiers Hollandais the following uniform: the coat was crimson with white collar, square lapels, turnbacks, cuffs and cuff slashes. The epaulettes were either scarlet or aurore. On each upper sleeve appeared crossed axes surmounted by a grenade. These were either white or yellow (see Plate 10E). The bearskin had a scarlet plume and white cords. The remainder of the dress was the same as described for the Grenadiers Francais.

Drummers

Again in the case of the drummers there is a mass of conflicting evidence available.

Firstly a uniform which is somewhat suspect but never the less is shown by a well known French artist M. Rigonaud, in his superb series of 'Plumet' prints. Possibly this only depicts the drummers of the band.

A bearskin is worn, without a plate, with white cords and flounders, a plume with the lower half sky blue and the upper half white and a yellow patch with a silver grenade.

The coat was sky blue with yellow collar, square lapels, turnbacks, cuffs and cuff flaps. The collar, lapels and cuffs (not the cuff flaps) were edged with white lace. The button holes on the lapels and pockets were edged with white lace brandenbergs and did not have a tassel or fringe. The vertical pockets were piped yellow and the two rear waist buttons were decorated with a white lace 'taille'.

The epaulettes were of scarlet wool and the remainder of the dress, breeches, etc, was the same as for the Grenadiers Francais.

The drum was also similar to the French having mid blue rims with painted yellow grenades in alternate triangles formed by zig-zag white lines (see Plate 10H). On the brass centre section between the white tensioning ropes appeared embossed grenades, alternately one then two.

According to the Alsace Collection, the drummers at first wore a crimson coat with white collar, lapels, cuffs, cuff flaps and turnbacks. Gold lace appeared on the collar, lapels and cuffs and gold lace to the lapel and pocket button holes. The pockets were piped white. Epaulettes were scarlet as was the plume in the bearskin. The bearskin patch was crimson with a gold grenade and the cords and flounders white. Remainder was as described above (see Fig 46C and Plate 10F).

After a contemporary print we find the drummer wearing an identical uniform to the men with the addition of gold lace to the collar, lapels and cuffs (no brandenbergs).

A further variation gives gold and crimson lace in place of the gold just mentioned and the bearskin had gold and crimson cords with a gold grenade on the crimson top patch.

In all the cases described it would appear that chin scales either brass or white metal were sometimes worn.

OPPOSITE: A: Drum Major, Grenadiers Hollandais, 1810. B: Sapeur, Grenadiers Hollandais. C: Drummer, Grenadiers Hollandais after the Alsace Collection. D: Musician, Grenadiers Hollandais, 1811. E. Negro, Grenadiers Hollandais, chapeau chenois. F: Drum Major, Chasseurs à pied. 1803.

Fig 46

A

B

C

D

E

F

Musicians

In the first instance the uniform of the musician is identical to the sky blue uniform which was described at the beginning of the section dealing with Grenadiers Hollandais drummers. The only minor differences are as follows. The silver lace brandenbergs on the lapels and pockets terminated in a fringe, and also the cuff slashes may have been white. In place of epaulettes silver trefoil shoulder straps were worn and these were on a yellow backing (see Plate 10G). At first a bicorne was worn with silver tassels, stiffeners and cockade strap. Scalloped silver lace edged the hat while at the extreme edge feather tufts were worn coloured white, red, sky blue, white red, etc. A panache of sky blue, white and red feathers appeared over the cockade with a white plume rising from the centre. Either turned down boots or Hussar style boots with silver lace and a silver tassel were worn. A light epée was carried on a white waist belt which passed under the flap of the breeches. Both waistcoat and breeches were white.

From 1811 a black fur colpack or busby replaced the bicorne. This had a yellow bag piped and tasseled silver. At the front a sky blue plume with a white tip rose from a white pom-pon (see Fig 46D). Another variation appears to be silver lace, etc, replaced with gold and the colpack sometimes worn with white cords around the front. The Leyden museum also quotes crimson in place of yellow facings with the gold lace.

According to Knotel, the musicians wore a light blue greatcoat with yellow piping to the collar and cuffs, and white trefoils on the shoulders. A plain black bicorne was worn with a white cockade strap.

The chapeau chinois (chinese hat) carrier wore a uniform of oriental cut. He had a sky blue sleeveless jacket with silver lace edging and embroidery, a sleeved yellow waistcoat with a silver laced yellow collar and silver lace on the pointed cuffs and front of the waistcoat. Around the waist a crimson sash was worn which tied at the left and terminated in silver fringes. The two front corners of the jacket had silver tassels attached to them. Baggy white mameluke trousers were worn over red leather boots.

On the head a scarlet fez or cap with scalloped silver lace at the top, which was encircled at the bottom by a white turban. At the front the turban was joined together by a gilt clip. A mameluke sword was carried on a crimson shoulder cord. The chapeau chinois itself was brass except for the ball which was blue with gilt stars (see Fig 46E).

Another variation shows the fez to be sky blue with a white plume and the braid to be yellow instead of silver. The boots were also yellow.

Bacquoy and Malibran show yet another variation on this dress and is detailed as follows:

White turban with a yellow metal buckle in the front centre, crimson fez body with a white zig-zag design around the top edge. The figure wears brass ear-rings. Yellow shirt with white lace. Pale blue waistcoat with white lace. Baggy white pantaloons, crimson shoes, crimson waist sash tied at the front with two tassels hanging down the front. White shoulder belt with brass buckle and slides, brass grenade badge (the buckle worn on the front), scimitar, with brass grip and bar, brass scabbard, attached to shoulder belt by white frog.

The instrument is the 'chapeau chinois' which has a black shaft and brass fittings between the top bell holder and the lower bell holder is a circular pale blue plate with a brass star in the centre. On top of the instrument is a gilt eagle.

Chasseurs à Pied

In many respects the Chasseurs à pied followed the styles of dress of the Têtes du Colonne of the Grenadiers. However, this section is limited to the basic full dress uniforms. For tenue de ville, etc, the styles worn by the Grenadiers should be used but with the obvious changes in colouring of plume, epaulettes and turnback ornaments.

Drum Major

The uniform described here is the full dress uniform of around 1803 (see Fig 46F and Plate 10J). The chapeau, worn 'on Bataille', was edged with gold lace and had gold tassels and a gold cockade strap. There does not appear to be any stiffeners. A 'panache' of ostrich feathers, coloured blue, white and red, when viewed from the front, had a dark green plume rising from the centre. The habit coat was dark blue with white pointed lapels and scarlet pointed cuffs. The turnbacks were scarlet as was the piping around the pockets. Gold lace was worn around the collar, top and bottom, around the lapels, turnbacks and down the sleeve seams. The scarlet pointed cuffs had two gold laces with scarlet showing between. Above the cuffs were two angled gold rank stripes. As with most musicians and drummers uniforms, a gold lace inverted 'W' appeared on the buttons at the rear. The pockets had gold lace inside the scarlet piping. The button holes on the lapels and pockets had gold lace brandenbergs with fringes. On the shoulders, scarlet swallows nests were worn, edging gold lace and with a gold fringe at the bottom. Gold epaulettes were worn, over the swallows nests. Gold horns and grenades appeared on the turnbacks. The waistcoat was white edged with gold lace. The waistbelt, worn over the waistcoat, was white, edged with gold and bearing a pattern of gold oak leaves. The belt plate was gilt and bore a hunting horn. The sabre of the drum major incorporated an eagle's head on the gilt hilt and was carried in a black leather scabbard, richly decorated with gilt. It was carried in a white leather frog edged with gold. The breeches were white with ornate gold lace 'spades' on the front. Short black boots were worn, laced and fringed with gold.

The drum major's shoulder belt was dark green with gold fringed edges and gold oak leaves, grenades and horns. Miniature drum sticks were carried in a gilt holder on the belt (see Plate 10K). White gloves with gauntlet cuffs were worn, the cuffs being fringed with gold. The drum major's baton was of natural wood with a silver head and heel, and gold cords. By 1808, the swallows nests would have disappeared and the short boots would be replaced by normal Hussar style boots edged with gold. In all probability, the 'spade' decorations would have been replaced by gold Hungarian knots and a gold lace stripe carried on the outside seams of the breeches.

The following comes again from Bacquoy and Malibran and describes the uniform worn around 1810:

Black cocked hat worn sideways, scalloped gold lace edging to hat, gold cockade loop and button, but no cockade, three small gold stays either side of loop, gold tassels at each end. A cluster of three small feathers above the loop, the outer two dark green, centre one red, raising from these is a long white feather, not a plume. The figure is also wearing gold earings.

Long tailed dark blue coat, blue collar laced top and front with scalloped gold lace, white lapels laced with scalloped gold lace and buttons. Red turnbacks, no ornaments on them. Scalloped gold lace seams back and front of sleeves and on the pockets. Gold epaulettes straps and fringes.

White waistcoat with gold buttons. White breeches with gold thigh ornaments. Black hessian boots with gold lace edging and tassels. Crimson belt with scalloped gold lace edging, a gold plate in the centre bearing two small ebony drum sticks in gold mounts. Gilt single bar guard to sabre, black grip, gold lace sword knot and strap, black scabbard with gilt ferrule, white sword frog which is attached to the bottom of the drum sash, gilt stud in the centre.

Brown mace, with silver top and green cords and tassels. Job shows a version of this uniform, as above with the following variations: The two small outer plumes are red within the centre on dark green, the hat also had a dark green fringe along the top edges. On the lapels are gold buttonhole fringes. The sword frog is gold with a gold fringe on the edges, boots are red with gold edging and tassels.

Sapeur

The sapeur in full dress wore a black bearskin, without a patch or plate. The cords and flounders were mixed gold, green and scarlet. The tassels at the front were white. Above the pom-pon cockade at the left side a green plume with a red tip was worn. The habit coat was blue with white pointed lapels, scarlet pointed cuffs piped white, and scarlet turnbacks. The pockets were piped scarlet. Around the collar, lapels, cuffs, turnbacks and pockets, and down the sleeve seams appeared gold and green lacing. This lacing appears inside the piping on the cuffs and pockets. On the turnbacks, crossed axes in gold appeared on a green patch.

The epaulettes had green straps, edged with gold, gold half moons and mixed gold and scarlet fringes. On the upper arms, crossed gold axes had a green edging. Breeches were white with white or black long gaiters. The waist belt plate had a hunting horn embossed on it. The pouch on the 'porte hache' carried a brass eagle (see Fig 47A).

Drummer

The variations of dress of the Chasseurs à pied closely followed those of the Grenadiers, therefore a brief description of the full dress uniform worn between 1804-10 is given below.

The bearskin, without front plate or top patch was black with white cords. The plume was red over dark green. The habit coat was identical to the normal Chasseurs coat with the addition of mixed green and gold lacing to the collar, lapels and cuffs, turnback edges and pockets.

The pockets also carried a scarlet piping at the extreme edges. On the rear waist the inverted 'W' (taille) appeared in gold and green lace. The button holes on the lapels and on the pockets had gold and green lace brandenbergs with gold fringes. Swallows nests of scarlet cloth appeared at the shoulders and were edged all around with gold and green lace (see Fig 47B). The epaulettes worn over the swallows nests consisted of a green shoulder strap, edged with gold and with three gold bars across. The half moons were green and the fringes mixed gold and green. Alternatively the epaulettes appeared without the three bars. The turnback horns and grenades were gold on a white patch (see Plate 10L).

The remainder of the uniform was identical to the Grenadiers. On the drum carriage, in place of a grenade, appeared a brass hunting horn above the drumstick holder which was also brass. The drum itself was of brass with brass hunting horns appearing between the tensioner ropes, alternatively one horn on the centre line then two horns, one towards each edge. The rims were mid blue, ornamented with painted yellow hunting horns. Another source shows the rims white with diagonal crosses. The one bar of each cross red, the other blue (see Plate 10I).

Musicians

While the basic descriptions of the uniform of the musicians agree, there are certain detail differences. Firstly the bicorne was identical for both uniforms and was edged with scalloped gold lace. The cockade strap, stiffeners and tassels were also gold. At the extreme edge appeared white and green tufts. The plume was white. The first coat was the standard Chasseur coat with gold lacing to the collar, lapels, cuffs and turnbacks. The turnback ornaments (horns and grenades) were gold. The pocket was outlined with scarlet piping. The epaulettes were identical to the Chasseurs but with half moons mixed gold and red. The retaining loops were green, edged gold. A light epée was carried on a white waist belt which passed under the trousers front flap. The sword knot was mixed green and gold. Waistcoat and breeches were the same as for the normal Chasseur. Black boots were worn with the tops turned down to show a fawn lining.

The second uniform attributed to the musicians of the Chasseurs had crimson cuffs, turnbacks and piping at the pockets. Gold lacing appeared as in the first description with the addition of gold lace to the pockets and a gold lace 'taille' at the waist (see Plate 10M).

The button holes on the lapels and pockets were ornamented with gold lace brandenbergs with fringes. In place of epaulettes, gold lace trefoils were worn on a crimson backing. The retaining straps were gold lined crimson. In place of boots, white gaiters are shown with this uniform (see Fig 47C).

Other details as for the first uniform.

The Fusiliers

The drum majors of the Fusiliers Grenadiers wore a black bicorne with gold lace edging, gold stiffeners, tassels, and cockade strap. Above the cockade a cluster of three ostrich feathers, light blue, white then scarlet (viewed from the front) with a white plume rising from the centre.

The normal coat of the Fusiliers Grenadiers was worn with the addition of gold lace to the collar, lapels, cuffs, turnbacks and pockets. The white cuff slashes carried a narrow gold piping. Turnback grenades were gold. The epaulettes were gold as were the two diagonal rank stripes on each arm. The white waistcoat was edged gold. Breeches were white and turned down boots were worn. The drum majors shoulder belt, which also supported a curved bladed sword, was scarlet, edged gold. Miniature drumsticks were carried in a gilt holder and a gilt grenade appeared above and below the holder. The baton was of natural wood with silver ornaments and cords.

I have been unable to trace any accurate information on the drum major of the Fusiliers Chasseurs.

Drummers

The drummers wore identical uniforms to the normal Fusilier with the addition of gold lace to the collar, lapels, cuffs, turnbacks and pockets. Turnback ornaments were gold. On the drum carriage, above the brass drumstick holder, appeared a brass grenade or hunting horn. The drums were brass with mid blue reins. The rims were either plain blue or had in the case of the Fusiliers Grenadiers gold painted grenades between the tensioner cords. In the case of the Fusiliers Chasseurs, gold painted hunting horns appeared on the lower rim, grenades on the top.

Sapeurs

In place of the normal shakos, the sapeurs of both regiments wore the bearskin. No plate or patch was worn. The cords and flounders were white in both cases. The Fusiliers Grenadiers wore scarlet plumes and Fusiliers Chasseurs green with scarlet tops. The remainder of their uniform was identical to their normal regiments, except that on each upper arm appeared crossed axes in white on red patches. Other sources show aurore axes without a patch. The brass waist belt plate worn over the apron had embosed on it a grenade for the Fusiliers Grenadiers and a hunting horn for the Chasseurs. It is probable that a more ornate uniform was worn on parade. In essence this was the same as already described with the addition of mixed scarlet gold lace, for the Fusiliers Grenadiers and green gold lace for the Fusiliers Chasseurs, to the collar, lapels, turnbacks, pockets and cuffs. On the sleeves the crossed axes were gold on scarlet patches, green for Fusiliers Chasseurs.

Epaulettes were as for the Grenadiers or Chasseurs as appropriate. Bearskins were also identical to the Grenadiers or Chasseurs.

The small pouch on the 'porte hache' had a brass eagle for both regiments.

Musicians

In theory there were no musicians for the Fusiliers regiments and it would appear that the Fusilier Chasseurs were in fact dependent on their parent regiment (Chasseur à pied) for their music. This may account for the fact that the uniform of a drum major for this regiment cannot be found.

However, the Fusiliers Grenadiers do appear to have had a band

Fig 47

ABOVE: A: Sapeur, Chasseurs à pied, 1805. B: Drummer, Chasseurs à pied, 1805. C: Musician, Chasseurs à pied. D: Drum Major, Fusiliers Grenadiers. E: Drummer, Fusiliers Grenadiers. F: Musician, Fusiliers Grenadiers.

and two versions of their uniform are described below.

In the first version the same uniform as the men was worn with the addition of gold lace to the collar and cuffs (not the cuff slashes) and with gold grenades on the turnbacks. The plume was white instead of red. Also gold trefoils were worn instead of epaulettes. In place of gaiters, Hussar style boots were worn without braiding or tassels. An epée was carried on a waistbelt worn under the flap of the breeches.

The second version, dated circa 1807 is identical with the addition of gold lace to the lapels, and turnbacks. In this instance the Hussar style boots were laced with gold and had gold tassels.

Marins de la Garde

There is no evidence to show the existence of sapeurs in the Battalion of Marines. There is, however, the unusual addition of trumpeters on foot in this unit. Their uniform was identical to the drummers so they are dealt with together. The shakos followed the pattern already laid down for the Marins except that for full dress the top and bottom bands were of gold lace. Cords and flounders were mixed scarlet and gold and the plume was scarlet. For tenue de campaign, the shako was laced aurore but the cords remained mixed scarlet and gold. For full dress wear the uniform was identical to the normal marins but in skyblue cloth with all braiding and lace mixed scarlet and gold. In place of the brass shoulder scales gold trefoils were worn on a scarlet base. The sabre peculiar to

---

BELOW: A: Drummer. Marins de la Garde, full dress. B: Trumpeter, Marins de la Garde, campaign dress. C: Musician, Marins de la Garde.

Fig 48

A   B   C

the battalion was carried on a black shoulder belt as previously described. The sword knot was mixed scarlet and gold. The drum was supported by a black leather drum carriage which had a brass drumstick holder. The apron was also of black leather. Each drummer had two sets of equipment, as did the men, one of soft black leather, the other varnished for parades. Some contemporary sources show the drum carriage and apron to be white but this is probably an error on the part of the artist.

The drum was of brass with blue rims. Tensioner cords were white. In the front centre, appeared an embossed eagle superimposed over an anchor. Carrying straps were black (white in the other case cited). The trumpet was brass with mixed gold and scarlet cords. On campaign, an identical blouse and trousers, as worn by the ordinary men was used but in sky blue cloth. The collar and cuffs were laced aurore. Musicians are shown wearing a bicorne hat with gold stiffeners, cockade strap and tassels. The plume was white. A habit coat was worn with pointed lapels and cuffs. The lapels, cuffs and turnbacks were scarlet. There was a gold lace edging to the collar, lapels and cuffs.

Gold anchors appeared on the turnbacks. On the shoulders gold lace trefoils were worn on a scarlet base. The button holes on the lapels were laced with gold brandenbergs ending in a point. The waistcoat was plain blue and blue Hussar breeches were worn with gold lace on the seams and gold knots at the front. Plain black boots 'a la Souvarov' were worn. An epée was carried on a black leather waist belt worn under the breeches flap. One source suggests the uniform of the drum major to be as that of the drummer or trumpeters but with double lace on the collar and the stripes of a 'maitre' on the sleeves. It is suggested that the shako plume would be white.

Sapeurs du Genie de la Garde

At first the drummers of the Sapeurs du Genie wore a uniform identical to the men but with aurore lace to the collar, lapels and cuffs. This was quickly superseded by gold lace to the collar, lapels, and cuffs and the turnback grenades also became gold. All lacing was inside the scarlet piping. Epaulettes and sword knots became the same as for sergeants. The crest and plume were also scarlet. The drum carriage was white with a brass grenade above the drumstick holder. The drum itself was similar to the Grenadiers, having embossed grenades. On the mid blue rims gold or yellow grenades were painted. Drummers shown in the Carl collection have gold lace brandenbergs on the button holes of the lapels. According to Fallou the lacing was a mixture of red and gold but this is not borne out by any other source.

It is doubtful if the Sapeurs had musicians but the Alsace collection shows figures reputed to be musicians of the Sapeurs Genie wearing the same uniform as the men. The collar, lapels and cuffs were bordered by gold lace and the cuffs themselves were scarlet in place of black. Instead of epaulettes gold trefoil shoulder straps were worn and an epée carried on a white waist belt worn under the trouser flap. Turned down boots are shown and the helmet has a white crest and plume.

Tirailleur Grenadiers

The sapeurs of the Tirailleur Grenadiers wore a bearskin identical to

Fig 48

D

E

F

*ABOVE: D: Drummer, Sapeurs Genie. E: Possible uniform of a musician
of the Sapeurs Genie. F: Sapeur Corporal of the Voltigeurs.*

that worn by the sapeurs of the Grenadiers à pied.

The remainder of their uniform was the same as the men of the regiment with the addition of mixed scarlet and gold lace to the collar, lapels, cuffs, pockets and turnbacks. This lace appeared inside the regulation piping. On the turnbacks appeared gold crossed axes, and on the upper arms the same emblem appeared, but larger, on a scarlet shaped patch. Equipment and the remainder of the dress was identical to that already described for sapeurs. The small pouch on the 'porte hache', however, only carried a brass crowned eagle and the belts were ornamented with the tetescle medusa.

Drummers

The drummers wore identical uniforms to the men with the addition of gold lace to the collar, lapels, cuffs and turnbacks. Only the sabre belt was worn. The drums were made of brass with mid blue rims and white tensioning ropes.

Tirailleurs Chasseurs

The sapeurs of the Tiralleurs Chasseurs wore the uniform as already described for Tirailleur Grenadiers but the epaulette strap was green and the fringes red. The bearskin was identical to that worn by the Chasseurs à pied.

Drummers

As already described for the men with gold lace to collar, lapels cuffs and turnbacks. Remainder as Tirailleur Grenadiers.

Voltigeurs

The sapeurs wore a black bearskin without plate, white cords with tassels falling on the right hand side, green over red plume, tricolour cockade at base of plume. Uniform as for the rest of the regiment, with two yellow metal crossed axes on each sleeve, green epaulettes and straps. White apron worn under the coat. Large white gauntlets, white cross belts with a brass grenade on the belt over the left shoulder and further down, near the waist, a disc similar to the medusa head ornament worn by the Grenadier sapeurs. White waistbelt with large brass belt plate.

Sapeur Sergeant

He has the stripes of his rank, no musket or pouch, two pistols carried in the waistbelt, they appear to be thrust through the belt, there is no visible means of securing them apparent. He has the normal guard sabre, otherwise dressed as the sapeur.

Drum Major

Black cocked hat, bordered with a gold lace band, with gold tufts along the top edges, gold cockade loop and button over tricolour cockade, three small gold retaining bars each side of the loop. Green plume with a red tip. Uniform as for the rest of the regiment but the coat has long tails and a gold lace border to the collar and lapels. Gold trefoil knots on the shoulders. No stripes of rank. White waistcoat with the edges and the pockets edged with gold lace, gold buttons. White breeches, Hungarian boots, black with gold lace and tassels. Large black gauntlets, white crossbelt with a narrow band of gold lace down each side, in the front centre a gold shield bearing two black miniature drum sticks, above this a gold grenade, gilt single bar guard to sabre, black grip, gold sword knot, black scabbard with gilt ferrule. Black staff with silver pommel and gold cords.

Drummers and Fifers

Uniform as for the rest of the regiment with a gold lace band on the top and front edges of the collar.

Tambour-Maitre

As the drummers corporals ranks stripes in aurore lace, black staff with brass pommel and red cords.

Musicians

Shako as for the rest of the regiment with white plume and ball tuft, uniform as for the regiment with gold lace edging to the collar and lapels, gold trefoil shoulder knots. White waistcoat and breeches. Black Hungarian boots with gold lace and tassels. Sabre has brass single bar guard and grip, scabbard black with brass ferrule, carried from a white waistbelt, worn around the waist and under the front flap of the breeches.

Grosse Caisse

Painted in blue and bearing a gold eagle between two wreaths painted in their natural green, white straps etc, the musician who plays it does not have an apron.

Tambour Long

Painted the same as the 'grosse caisse' with the same ornaments. Cymbals player has large black gauntlets.

Conscrit Grenadiers

The bearskin of the sapeurs was identical to that of the Grenadiers à pied. The remainder of the uniform was as for the men of the Conscrit Grenadiers but with gold crossed axes on the turnbacks. On the upper arms red crossed axes edged gold appeared. The epaulettes were scarlet edged gold with gold half moons and mixed red and gold fringes. On the 'porte hache' belt appeared brass crossed axes, surmounted by a brass grenade.

Drummers

As for the men but with yellow or gold lace to collar, and six inverted yellow or gold lace chevrons on the sleeves. The Musée de l'Armee also cites the following for drummers and Fifers:

Uniform as the men but with aurore lace to the collar, lapels and cuffs. From the Wurtz Collection comes the following descriptions of the drum major and musicians of the Conscrit Grenadiers.

Tambour Maitre

Black colback with a red bag, laced on edges and centre with aurore lace also aurore tassel. Red plume in front centre. Uniform of the drum major: Cross belt carries the sabre and has a brass grenade on it. Brown staff with brass pommel.

Musicians

Shako was as for the rest of the regiment, with a white plume in the front centre, raising from a crimson ball. Blue coat as for the regiment, with blue collar, crimson lapels and cuffs, white cuff slashes, aurore lace on the top and front of collar, around lapels and cuffs. Aurore or gold trefoil shoulder straps. Crimson turnbacks. White waistcoat and breeches. Black boots with fawn turn down tops. Brass hilt and guard to sabre, brass scabbard, carried from a white cross belt.

The Grasse Caise was painted blue and bore a golden eagle between two green wreaths. The musician who played it had a white apron and a large white gauntlet. The cymbals player, had large white gauntlets. The triangle player was dressed in musicians' uniform but was either a dwarf or a child, probably the latter and probably the son of one of the musicians.

Conscrit Chasseurs

The bearskin of these sapeurs was identical to that worn by the sapeurs of the Chasseurs à pied. The uniform was identical to the men's but with gold crossed axes on the turnbacks and epaulettes with green, gold edged, straps, gold half moons and mixed red and gold fringes. On the upper arms appeared red crossed axes piped with gold. The 'porte hache' belt carried brass crossed axes surmounted by a brass hunting horn. The gaiters were of light infantry pattern with green edging and tassels.

Fig 49

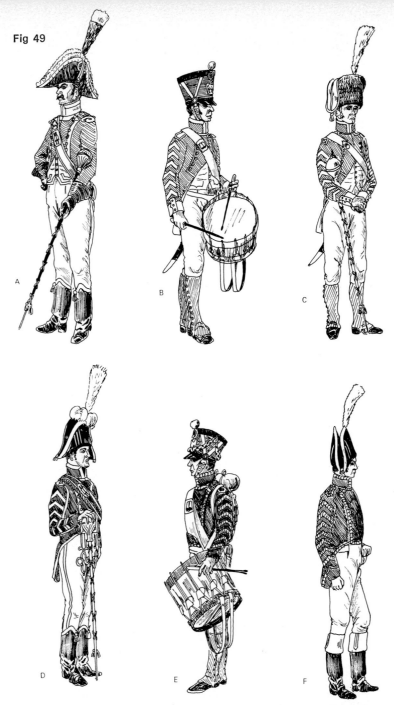

ABOVE: A: Drum Major, Voltigeurs. B: Drummer, Conscrits Grenadiers. C: Tambour Maitre, Conscrits Grenadiers. D: Drum Major, Pupilles. E: Drummer, Pupilles. F: Musician, Pupilles.

Remainder of equipment as described previously. Drummers were as for Conscrit Grenadiers.

Gardes Nationales de la Garde

The bearskin of the sapeur was identical to that worn by the Chasseurs à pied.

The uniform was identical to that worn by the Grenadiers of the National Guard with the addition of mixed red and gold lace to the collar, lapels and cuffs. Red grenades appeared on the turnbacks. On the upper arms appeared red crossed axes piped gold. The remainder was as standard for the sapeurs.

Drummers

Though the Gardes Nationales were organised on Line Regiment principles, they did not, as was the Line practice, have hornists in the Voltigeurs companies.

Consequently all companies had drummers which were dressed as the men with the addition of gold lace to the collar, lapels and cuffs. The drums, etc, were identical to those of the Tirailleur Grenadiers.

Pupilles de la Garde

The youth who was the drum major of the Pupilles was about 5 feet 2 inches tall and wore a black bicorne edged with gold braid, and gold stiffeners and cockade strap. Above the cockade a white plume rose from a panache of three green ostrich feathers. The coat was green with gold lacing down the seams of the sleeves, front and rear, and the back seams of the coat. The collar, lapels, turnbacks, shoulder straps, cuffs and pockets were edged with gold lace. Above each cuff appeared two gold inverted chevrons showing the rank of sergeant major and above these on each arm appeared seven gold lace inverted chevrons. The breeches were white and gold lace strips down the outside seams and gold lace Austrian knots on the fronts. Short black Hussar type boots were worn with a gold edging and gold tassels. Across the right shoulder the cross belt was worn and was green with edging of gold lace and gold lace fringes. A light epée, shorter than usual, was carried with a gilt hilt and a gold lace sword knot.

The drum major's baton was of natural wood with a silver head, ferrule and cords.

Drummers and Fifers

These wore identical uniforms to the men but with mixed gold and green lace to the collar, cuffs and lapels. This mixed gold and green lace also appeared on the arms in the form of seven evenly spaced inverted chevrons which went from the front to the back seams of the arm. The cords and flounders on the shako were also mixed gold and green. The drums etc, were as described for the Tirailleur Grenadiers.

Musicians

The musicians uniform was the same as described for the drummers but a bicorne with gold lace edging, gold stiffeners, tassels and cockade strap was worn. It is probable that a white plume was also worn.

5: Eagles and Colours of the Imperial Guard

WITHIN a month of the proclamation of his Empire on May 18, 1804, Napoleon had decided upon its emblem. Rejecting a cock and then a lion, he had selected an Eagle with spread wings and at once commissioned designs for the Great Seal of State and for the emblems of his Army and Navy. To the Army he announced a ceremony at which new Standards and Colours would be presented by himself. A few days later, he made plain the relation of the Eagle emblem to the Standard or Colour (or 'flag'). Writing to Marshal Berthier, he emphasised that the Eagle was to be the essential and priceless symbol of France and the Empire, while the 'flag' below was to be of less importance and might be replaced as necessary.

During the period of the Empire, two models of Eagle were produced. The master-pattern of the first in 1804, was the fine work of Chaudet, a well-known sculptor. Replicas were cast in bronze and ormolu-gilded; each stood almost 8 inches high and was fastened to a plinth 2 inches deep. To attach the Eagle to its staff, a tubular socket $2\frac{1}{2}$ inches long was soldered beneath the plinth. The entire emblem was therefore just over 12 inches high. Metal numerals indicating the number of the regiment within its arm were attached to the plinth, front and rear. (It has been suggested by some authorities that Guard Eagles bore, instead of a number, a badge indicating the arm, eg, a grenade for Grenadier units. Although this is not unlikely it is not proven by the one example known today: that of the Grenadiers à cheval). In all, each 1804 Eagle weighed just over 4 pounds. The second model of Eagle was produced very rapidly in 1815. Due mostly to this urgency, it was less finely moulded than its predecessor though entirely similar in general form.

Standards, Guidons and Colours

Amongst European armies of the day, the Eagles of the French were unique in their position *vis-à-vis* the 'flag'. The Eagle was always referred to as 'l'Aigle'; the flag on the other hand was described by one of the three following terms:

'Drapeau' (or Colour). Carried by infantry and dismounted arms, it was usually a large square flag.

'Etendard' (or Standard). Carried by heavy cavalry, it was square but usually rather smaller than the typical Colour.

'Guidon' (also Guidon in English). Carried by some light cavalry and artillery. It was swallow-tailed and usually about the same dimensions as a Standard.

Eagles and their attendant 'flags' of Guard units were always carried by a sous-lieutenant or lieutenant. This contrasted with the Line regulation in force until 1808 under which the Eagle was carried by the senior sergeant-major.

Lodging of Eagles

An order had been issued in October 1802 that the Colours, Standards and Guidons of the Consular Guard should be permanently lodged in the Tuileries Palace. Under the Empire, this order continued in effect and the Eagles of the Guard were normally kept in the room next to the Throne Room. They were only withdrawn for state occasions and grand reviews, and to be taken into the field on active service. The latter was not however the invariable practice, as is shown below.

The Champ de Mars—December 5, 1804

It had been laid down that an Eagle (and an accompanying 'flag') was to be given to every battalion and squadron of the army. On this basis, out of a total of 909 emblems for the whole army, the Guard was entitled to sixteen. In the event, thirteen were presented at the ceremony at the Champ de Mars on December 5, 1804. Every unit had to send its commanding officer with a delegation, for infantry of four officers and ten under-officers and soldiers per battalion. For the infantry of the Guard, deputations from four battalions of Grenadiers à pied and Chasseurs à pied received Eagles and Colours. Unfortunately, none of these emblems have survived to the present day, nor is there any reliable description or drawing. However, the Bataillon de Marins received its Eagle during 1805 and the Colour presented at the same time is still preserved today in France. From its design those of the Grenadiers and Chasseurs may at any rate be guessed.

The 1804 pattern Colour of the Bataillon de Marins

This is basically the regulation pattern Colour, a single sheet of silk 2 feet 8 inches (81 cm) square. On both sides the central diamond is white. The surrounding triangles in the other two national colours, blue and red, are arranged in pairs opposite each other: thus, the upper triangles on the mast and lower on the fly are blue, while the others are red. On the face, within the white diamond, is the salutation:

L'EMPEREUR

DES FRANCAIS,

AU B^{LON} DE MARINS

DE LA GARDE

IMPERIALE

On the reverse, beneath an imperial crown, an eagle clutching a thunder-

bolt in its talons is superimposed on an anchor. The word VALEUR
ET . . . DISCIPLINE are arranged in either side of this motif. In all four
corners on each side, there is an anchor within a wreath of leaves. Like
all Colours at this period, this one was covered with an oil based trans-
parent film the purpose of which was partly to protect the silk fabric,
and partly to give a durable surface on which embellishment could be
painted. These were all executed in gold and shaded with brown to give
an impression of depth. The Colour was nailed with gilt headed studs
to a blue wooden staff, 3 cm (or 1·18 inches) in diameter and 2 m 10 cm
(or 6 feet 10 inches) long including the Eagle at the top.

The 1806 Expansion

A decree issued on April 15, 1806 increased the Grenadiers and
Chasseurs from one regiment of three battalions each to three regiments
in each arm. Two regiments in each case were composed of veterans
and were called the 1er Regiment de Grenadiers à Pied, the 2eme
Regiment . . . etc; the third, as the junior battalion had been, was of
young soldiers or 'Velites'. All the regiments consisted of two battalions
but the Velites were not entitled to Eagles and never received them.
The Eagles and Colours presented in 1804 to the original two battalions
of each arm were now probably used by the battalions of each First
Regiment. It is very doubtful whether the Second Regiments ever
received emblems, even though the establishment of 'Porte-drapeau'
had been increased appropriately to four for each arm. In any case, the
expansion was brief for in October 1808 the Emperor ordered a reduc-
tion of each arm to a single regiment of two battalions.

In support of the contention that the short-lived Second Regiments of
each arm did not receive Eagles, is the known fact that in November
1807, the Guard still possessed only nineteen. In 1806, the City of
Paris had decided to present gold wreaths to units of the French Army
which had taken part in the previous year's victorious campaign in
Germany. A ceremony was organized on the outskirts of the City and
here the returning Imperial Guard arrived on November 25, 1807.
Nineteen Eagles were dipped to receive gold wreaths; amongst them it
is almost certain that the only infantry ones were those of the First Grenadiers and First Chasseurs, and probably that of the Marins. Strangely,
few subsequent reports mention these wreaths and not a single one
remains today although a total of 372 had been manufactured.

The 1810-1811 Expansion

On September 13, 1810, with the annexation of Holland, the Grenadier
regiment of the Dutch Royal Guard entered the Imperial Guard as the
2eme Regiment de Grenadiers à Pied, or 'Grenadiers Hollandais'.
Eight months later it was renumbered the Third Regiment when, under the
Decree of May 18, 1811, the Second (French) Regiments of the Grenadiers and Chasseurs were raised once again. Each of these new Regiments
received one Eagle and Colour, the Grenadiers Hollandais on June 30,
and the 2eme Grenadiers and 2eme Chasseurs on August 15, 1811. At
the same time the First Regiment of Grenadiers, and probably also that
of Chasseurs, received at least one new Colour. Although this may have
been because the old ones were worn out, replacements were of course

made necessary by the change in title from 'The Regiment' of 1804 to the 'First Regiment' of 1810. Of all the Colours presented during 1811, only those of the First and Second Regiments of Grenadiers still survive. There is little doubt that all were similar to these two which are described below.

The 1811 pattern Colours of the Grenadiers

In size and general design, these colours are the same as the 1804 pattern. But instead of the grenade, anchor or other badge within the wreath in each corner, there was now a numeral indicating the regimental number. There is wording on both sides, but the large badge incorporating the Eagle has disappeared. On the face, the salutation has been re-phrased and, for the First Grenadiers, now reads:

GARDE
IMPERIALE.
L'EMPEREUR
DES FRANCAIS
AU IER REGIMENT
DES GRENADIERS
A PIED

The wording on the reverse, probably unchanged from 1804, is:

VALEUR
ET DISCIPLINE.
IER BATAILLON

The Colour of the Second Regiment of Grenadiers is the same except for a change of numeral in the corners. In line five of the salutation on the face of the Colour, the numeral reads '2ME'.

Reductions in the Numbers of Eagles

In 1804, as we have seen, it was ordered that an Eagle was to be issued to every battalion and squadron. With up to five battalions in some Line regiments, this was an expensive exercise. Perhaps, therefore, it was as an economy measure that the principle of one Eagle per regiment was introduced. Discussed for several years by the Emperor and others, it was not established as a regulation until December 25, 1811. Though by no means uniform throughout the army, the effect in general was that a 1st Battalion or 1st Squadron retained its Eagle and carried it on behalf of the whole regiment. The remaining Eagles and accompanying 'flags' were returned to regimental depots.

The depots of the Guard were in or around Paris and, unlike the Line, Guard Regiments were generally in their depots when not actually engaged on operations. Their Eagles were lodged centrally in the Tuileries Palace. The decision to reduce the number of Eagles had its effect on the Guard in two ways. First with the scale of issue: in 1804 the infantry received one Eagle per battalion; in 1811, only one Eagle was issued to each new regiment. It is interesting that the Colour issued with each regimental Eagle still carried the inscription 'Ier BATAILLON'. This could have been intended to confirm that the Colour was to be carried by the 1st Battalion, or it might simply have been that the civil

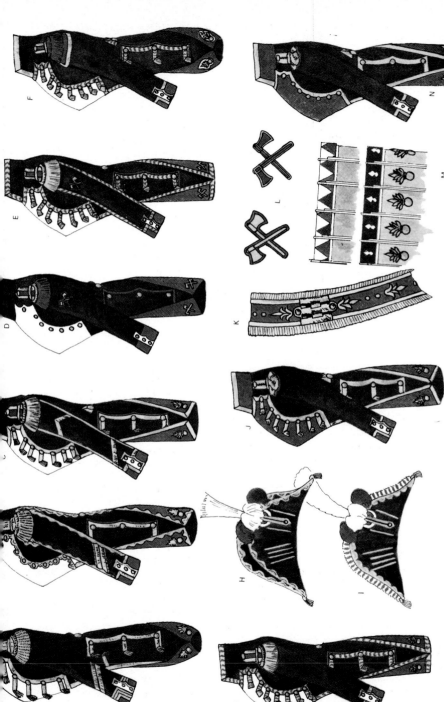

Plate 9: Têtes du Colonne, Grenadiers à pied

Key on page 113

servant responsible for ordering them omitted to make this change from the original design. Secondly, with the number of Eagles taken into the field on operations: all went on the 1805 campaign, but gradually the number was reduced as the years went by. For example it is known that the Marins left their Eagle in Paris during 1807. Which Eagles were taken to Spain in 1808 is not clear, but it is very likely that only one accompanied each regiment in the 1809 campaign in Germany. For the 1812 campaign instructions were specific: 'The Chasseurs à pied as an arm shall bring only one Eagle and similarly the arm of Grenadiers only one Eagle; these are always to be carried by the First Old Guard Regiment of each arm' wrote the Emperor in March. The Grenadiers' Colour was the one issued in 1811 and described above. Needless to say both those taken to Russia were safely brought back again together with the precious Eagles.

The Change to the Tricolour

For years the Emperor had wished to develop some way of displaying on a unit's Colour or Standard the names of battles in which it had taken part. With the restrictions imposed by the design of the 1804 pattern Colour, this was impossible. All sorts of shapes and designs, some even with new colours such as green, were suggested but none pleased him. In the end an obscure official named Barnier proposed the solution. He pointed out that the flag flown over the Tuileries when the Emperor was in residence was a simple tricolour. Such a design imposed none of the restrictions on embellishments that made the 1804 pattern so unsuitable for Napoleon's ideas. The proposal was made on February 9, 1812 and accepted immediately by the Emperor; the first orders for the manufacture of new Colours and Standards were signed the next day. Deliveries to the Line regiments began in April.

The reasons are not known, but the Guard kept its 1804 pattern Colours and Standards until 1813 when it was decided that the new type would be issued to units in possession of an Eagle. For the infantry, this meant the First and Second Grenadiers, the First and Second Chasseurs and the Marins. Almost certainly each received only one Colour; of the five only two exist today, those of the First and Second Grenadiers and these are described below.

The 1812 pattern Colour of the Second Grenadiers

This is very similar to a Line infantry Colour, being the same shape, size and general design (see page 114). It is square, measuring 2 feet 8 inches (or 82 cm) on each side. The colours were arranged with blue nearest the staff, then white, and red on the fly. A gold fringe about 1 inch (or 25 mm) wide goes all round, being stitched in between the two thicknesses of silk of which the Colour is made. To fasten it to the staff, a sleeve was sewn on to the 'blue' side and two cords provided to secure it at top and bottom. Above the Colour a broad tricolour ribbon of silk 3 feet 10 inches (or 1 m 20 cm) long and known as the cravat was tied, secured with a gold cord. The cravat was embroidered and fringed with gold, and its cord ended in two large tassels.

The pattern of embroidery around the edges of both sides of the Colour was, with one exception, common to all units whether Guard or

Line. The difference lay in the central wreaths top and bottom which for the Line were like the wreaths in the centre of either side and contained an 'N'. The Grenadiers of the Guard, however, while they had the N on either side, displayed a grenade at top and bottom. It is more than likely that other Guard units similarly displayed the badge of their arm.

The salutation on the face of the Colour was standard, Guard units having the words 'Garde Imperiale' above it. Thus for the Second Grenadiers, it reads:

GARDE
IMPERIALE
L'EMPEREUR
NAPOLEON
AU 2ME REGIMENT
DES GRENADIERS
A PIED

On the reverse are the following names:

MARINGO, ULM,
AUSTERLITZ, JENA,
EYLAU, FRIEDLAND,
ECKMÜHL, ESSLING,
WAGRAM, SMOLENSK,
MOSCOWA, —
VIENNE, BERLIN
MADRID, MOSCOU

All Guard Colours and Standards bore the same titles. Regiments of the Line on the other hand were restricted to a maximum of eight, the names of those battles since Ulm at which each had been present.

The Colour of the First Grenadiers is in the French Army Museum in Paris. It is exactly the same as that of the Second Grenadiers except of course for the number 'IER' in the fifth line of the salutation. It was this Colour that Napoleon kissed as he bid farewell to the Guard at Fontainebleu on April 20, 1814 after his Abdication. All the other Colours of the Guard were destroyed during or shortly after the debacle.

The Elba Colour

In his exile to Elba, Napoleon was permitted to take a small volunteer Guard of horse and foot. The infantry were known as the 'Bataillon Napoleon' and consisted of 608 Grenadiers and Chasseurs of the Old Guard. The unit was given an Eagle and a special Colour which was white with a diagonal red stripe on which three bees were emblazoned in gold.

The Colours of 1815

In June 1815, only a little over two weeks before Waterloo, a grand parade took place in Paris at which Eagles and Colours were once again presented to the Army. Two only went to the infantry of the Guard, to the First Regiments of Grenadiers and Chasseurs; the Marins received no Eagle doubtless because their establishment was now only that of a company. Unfortunately, both the infantry Colours were destroyed in 1815 as were five of the other six 'flags' and all the Eagles issued to

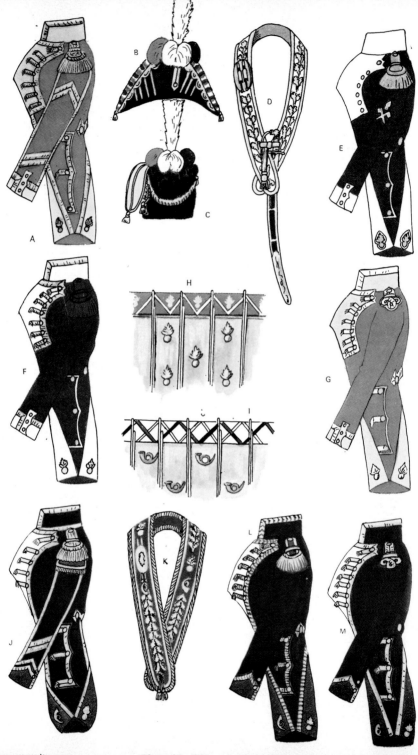

Plate 10: Têtes du Colonne

A   B   C

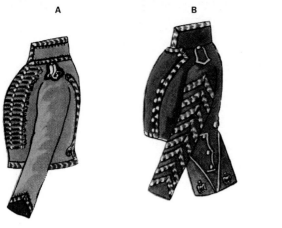

Plate 11
A. Trumpeter/Drummer, Marins de la Garde. B. Drummer, Pupilles de la Garde.
C. Drummer, Sapeurs du Genie de la Garde.

Key to Colour Plate 1, Page 33. Habit coats. 1. Grenadier, 1801-1808. 2. Caporal, 1808-1810. 3. Sergeant, 1811-1815. 4. Surtout of Fourrier. 5 and 6. Bearskin plates under the Consular Guard and under the Imperial Guard. 7-9. Bearskins of Grenadier, NCO and Officer. 10 Pom-pon cockade. 11. Bearskin patch. 12. Grenadier bicorne. 13. Shoulder strap of the velites. 14. Officers' and NCOs' turnbacks. 15. Bonnet de police.

Key to Colour Plate 2, page 36: Habit coats. 1. Chasseur, 1801-1808. 2. Chasseur, 1808-1810. 3. Caporal, 1811-15. 4. Surtout of Sergeant. 5-7. Bearskins of Chasseur Sergeant and rear view of Chasseur bearskin. 8 and 12. Turnback horn and grenade detail. 9 and 10. Detail of NCOs' flounder and cords. 11. Chasseur sword knot.

Key to Colour Plate 4, page 40: 1. Paletot of Marin. 2 and 3. Side and front views of Marins shako. 4. Paletot of Contre-Maitre. 5. Brass scale shoulder strap. 6. Detail of NCO's lace and braid. 7. Officers' coat. 8. Senior Officers' coat. 9. Cuff of Quartier-Maitre. 10. Cuff of Marin.

Key to Colour Plate 9, page 109: A. Drum Major, 1804. B. Drum Major, 1808. C. Tambour Maitre. D. Sapeur, 1803. E. Sapeur, Full Dress, 1810. F. Drummer, 1804. G. Drummer. 1809. H. Chapeau of Drum Major. I. Chapeau of Musician. J. Musician, 1800. K. Drum Majors' arm ornaments. L. Sapeurs' arm ornaments. M. Drum rims, upper: Consular Guard, lower: Imperial Guard. N. Musician according to Marco de St Hilaire, 1810.

Key to Colour Plate 10, page 112: A. Drum Major, Grenadiers Hollandais. B. Chapeau of the Drum Major until 1811. C. Colpack worn after 1811. D. Drum Majors belt and sabre, Grenadiers Hollandais. E. Sapeur after the Carl Collection, Grenadiers Hollandais. F. Drummer after the Alsace Collection, Grenadiers Hollandais. G. Musician, Grenadiers Hollandais. H. Drum rim. Grenadiers Hollandais. I. Drum rim Chasseurs à pied. J. Drum Major, Chasseurs à pied, 1803. K. Drum Majors' belt, Chasseurs à pied. L. Drummer, Chasseurs à pied. M. Musician, Chasseurs a pied.

Key to Colour Plate 12, page 116: 1. Colour of the Bataillon de Marins de la Garde 1805-1813 (reverse). 2. Fanion of a battalion of the 1er Voltigeurs de la Garde (reverse). (The face is probably exactly the opposite, ie with the 'N' back to front and the grenades and horns in opposite corners, and positions). 3. Detail of cravat-end and tasselled cords of 1812 pattern Colours. 4. Porte-aigle of the Marins de la Garde (after Suhr), c. 1806. 5. Porte-aigle of the 1st Grenadiers (after Raffet), c. 1814.

LEFT: Colour of the 1ER Grenadiers à pied de la Garde, 1811-1813 (face). This Colour was carried to Moscow and back.

RIGHT: Colour of the 2ME Grenadiers à pied de la Garde, 1813-1814 (face).

the Guard. The only emblem saved and still preserved today is the Standard of the Horse Artillery. We can therefore only guess at the design of the Colours of the Grenadiers and Chasseurs. However, we have already seen that the Eagle was much the same as in 1804; its staff was blue, and below it we know that there was a cravat and gold cords similar to the 1812 pattern.

For the Line, the new Colours and Standards were once more basically the tricolour but simpler and much larger. A Colour was 3 feet 10 inches (or 1 m 20 cm) square and made of a double thickness of silk. It had only a fine gold fringe, and a narrow design of leaves embroidered close to the edge. The inscriptions, embroidered on cut-out black cloth, were simple. On the face:

L'EMPEREUR
NAPOLEON
AU M̲E̲
REGIMENT
D'INFANTERIE
DE LIGNE

and on the reverse the titles of battles at which the regiment had been present.

The Standard of the Guard Horse Artillery is 2 feet 8½ inches square, and, apart from the inscriptions, very similar to the 1812 pattern; it has an 'N' in each of the four wreaths on both sides. The extraordinary thing is that it has no salutation, nor indeed any indication at all of ownership. It bears simply the names of battles and foreign cities though some of the latter are strange and quite out of historical sequence. On the face of the Standard are:

MARENGO. ULM
AUSTERLITZ JENA
EYLAU. FRIEDLAND
WAGRAM.
LA MOSKOWA
LUTZEN MONTMIRAIL

and on the reverse:

VIENNE, BERLIN
MADRID, MILAN
MOSCOW, VARSOVIE
VIENNE, LE CAIRE

It is very probable that all the six Colours and Standards of Guard units made and used during the 100 Days were exactly the same as the one surviving example described above.

Pennons (or Fanions)

No infantry regiment of the Middle or Young Guards was issued with an Eagle or a Colour. Nearly all of these units belonged either to the corps of Grenadiers or to the Chasseurs and in a sense therefore bore allegiance through the Eagles of these arms. However, there is no doubt that most or all of these junior regiments possessed battalion pennons though unfortunately little evidence of their size, design or colour remains today. These should not of course be confused with the streamers (or

Plate 12

Key on page 11

1

VALEUR ET DISCIPLINE

2

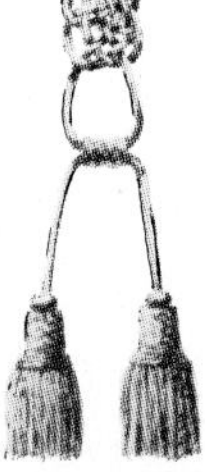

3

4

5

banderoles) attached to the halberds carried, at any rate in the Line infantry, by the escorts to Eagles. These streamers were generally anything up to about 24 inches long by 8 inches deep and were pointed or swallow-tailed; fanions on the other hand were square or oblong in shape.

In a letter to Bessieres (Commander of the Imperial Guard) on March 10, 1812, Napoleon ordered that every Guard battalion was to have a fanion, red for Voltigeurs and white for Tirailleurs. He added that their design was to give no indication of a unit's identity nor its membership of the Guard. How strictly this was obeyed is not known but certainly some fanions were embroidered in gold with the words 'Garde Imperiale'. Only one still exists (in Russia) and has been identified with reasonable certainty as having belonged to a battalion of the 1er Voltigeurs. It is almost square, 26 inches × 26½ inches and is red with an edging of white braid; in the middle a white 'N' is surrounded with green fronds and surmounted by a white eagle bearing a yellow crown; in two corners are white grenades, in the other two white hunting horns. At the top of its staff is a spear-head and attached to it are tasselled white cords.

Two other pennons should be mentioned: one (in Vienna) is white with a crowned eagle in the middle and alternate grenades and hunting horns in the corners. Within each horn is the number 13, painted like the other embellishments in gold. This pennon may perhaps have belonged to the 13ME Tirailleurs. The other appears in the *Bourgeois de Hambourg*, a book of on-the-spot-sketches made by Christopher Suhr between 1806 and 1815: Plate 91 shows a group of Marins de la Garde, one of whom carries an Eagle on a pale blue staff. Below the Eagle and instead of a conventional Colour there is a pale violet pennon which seems to be about 12 inches square. It has a gold fringe and gold (or yellow) badges on it which may be bees or anchors. There is also a double gold cord with flounders and tassels. What this pennon may have been is open to conjecture.

There seems to be no contemporary evidence at all of what fanions, if any, were carried by battalions of Grenadiers and Chasseurs.

Eagles and Pennons on Parade

We have already described how the Eagle bearers of the Foot Grenadiers and Chasseurs of the Old Guard were lieutenants or sous-lieutenants. The Eagle of the Marins on the other hand seems to have been carried by a sous-officier, a maitre or a contre maitre. Their uniforms were no different from those of others of their rank, though it is worth remembering that they were usually old soldiers often wearing the cross of the Legion d'Honneur.

To support the Eagle, its bearer wore a Colour belt. Unfortunately there is little reliable contemporary evidence of what these belts looked like and the following descriptions are therefore largely the author's deductions:

The Grenadiers and Chasseurs usually wore a plain white belt in all orders of undress. In full dress a red leather belt edged with gold braid was worn by Grenadier Eagle bearers (see cover illustration) and a similarly braided green leather belt by Chasseurs. In addition, for grand parades on special occasions, it seems likely that at least the First Grenadiers possessed a crimson belt with a gold fringe and embroidered embellishments (see Plate 12). The Marins Eagle bearer on the other hand wore a polished black leather belt in all orders of dress (see Plate 12). Belts were worn over the left shoulder by all Eagle bearers.

When carried on the march, Eagles (and their Colours) were usually protected by a black oilskin cover, or 'case'.

Position of Emblems on Parade

The Eagle was always escorted by two senior NCOs who were probably sergeants specially selected because of their proven courage in action. The position was coveted and also of course particularly exposed in battle: for this reason escorts in Line infantry regiments were eventually given a special uniform including; spectacularly, a helmet. No such provision was however made for the Old Guard: the escorts to its Eagles were simply old soldiers with no special distinction of dress or arms. It is, however, likely that on parade, the escorts carried muskets without bayonets to prevent the possibility of a colour becoming snagged and torn. The two escorts marched on either side of the Eagle bearer.

When a battalion was formed in line, its Eagle was placed in the centre of the front rank. In column, the Eagle was mid-way along the column and, in action, in the centre file.

Battalion pennons, on the other hand, were carried on the right flank in line, or at the head when in column. The pennon was fastened to a baton, sometimes with an imitation spearhead at its tip, which was plugged into the muzzle of its bearer's musket. Pennons were carried by sous-officiers, usually sergeants.

Conclusion

The main purpose of this chapter has been to give the reader accurate descriptions of Eagles and those Guard Infantry Colours that are still preserved today. An additional object has been to provide other evidence in parallel which will, we hope, enable the reader to decide for himself the design of those Colours we have been unable to describe. In that, as with any matter of history for which there is no adequate contemporary evidence, it is worth emphasising that no answer logically reached can be declared wrong.

Appendix 1: Rank Equivalents

French	Marins de la Garde	English
Colonel	Capitaine de vaisseau	Colonel
Major		Lt Colonel
Chef de bataillon	Capitaine de fregate	Major
Capitaine	Lieutenant de vaisseau	Captain
Lieutenant *	Enseigne de vaisseau	Lieutenant
Sergent-major	Maitre	Sergeant-Major
Sergent	Contre-Maitre	Sergeant
Fourrier		Quartermaster Sergeant
Caporal	Quartier-Maitre	Corporal
Soldat (Sapeur)	Matelot	Private
Tambour-major		Drum Major
Tambour-maitre		Drum master
Tambour (Trompette)		Drummer (Trumpeter)

* Note the rank of sous-lieutenant was not normally used by the Guard.

Appendix 2: Officers' Rank Distinctions

THE method of indicating the officer's rank in the Guard followed the same pattern as that used by the Line. That is the type and positioning of the epaulettes.

The colonel wore two gold epaulettes with the fringes of thick gold cord. The majors wore similar epaulettes but with the shoulder straps covered in silver lace in place of gold. The chefs de bataillon wore a gold epaulette with thick gold fringes on the left shoulder and a gold contra-epaulette (ie, no fringes) on the right shoulder.

Capitaines were distinguished in the same manner as the chefs de bataillon but the epaulette on the left shoulder was fringed with fine gold cords. Adjutants had the same distinctions as the capitaines but the positions were reversed. That is the epaulette on the right shoulder and the contra-epaulette on the left. Lieutenants were identical to the capitaines but in some instances Line practice was followed and a thin red silk stripe appeared on the shoulder straps.

The rank distinctions of the NCOs are given fully in the text.

Appendix 3: Formation of Units

TABLE showing the dates of formation of the Guard regiments in chronological order and the dates of disbandment.

Grenadiers à pied
1st Regiment created December 2, 1799 —disbanded
September, 1815.
2nd Regiment created April 15, 1806—merged with the
1st Regiment 1808; reformed May 18, 1811 and disbanded
September 2, 1815.
Grenadiers Hollandais became the 2nd Regiment on
September 13, 1810—became the 3rd Regiment May 18, 1811
with the formation of a second French regiment—disbanded
February 15, 1813.
3rd Regiment (French) was formed on April 8, 1815 and
disbanded September 24, 1815.
4th Regiment was formed May 9, 1815 and disbanded
September 24, 1815.

Chasseurs à pied
1st Regiment created December 2, 1799 as 'light
infantry'—became Chasseurs 1801—disbanded
October 11, 1815.
2nd Regiment created April 15, 1806; merged with 1st
Regiment 1808—reformed May 18, 1811—disbanded
October 11, 1815.
3rd Regiment created April 8, 1815—disbanded
October 1, 1815.
4th Regiment created May 9, 1815—disbanded
October 1, 1815.
Compagnie des Veterans created July 12, 1801,
continued under the Monarchy.

Marins
Created September 17, 1803, disbanded April 23,
1814 (one company went to Elba with Napoleon)
reformed April 8, 1815—disbanded September 4, 1815.
Velite Grenadiers created July 29, 1804.
Velite Chasseurs created July 29, 1804.
Fusilier Chasseurs created October 19, 1806—
disbanded May 12, 1814.
Fusilier Grenadiers created December 15, 1806—
disbanded May 12, 1814.

Tirailleur-Grenadiers
1st Regiment created January 16, 1809 became 1st
Tirailleurs December 30, 1810.
2nd Regiment created April 25, 1809—became 2nd
Tirailleurs December 30, 1810.

Tirailleur-Chasseurs
1st Regiment created January 16, 1809—became 1st
Voltigeurs December 30, 1810.
2nd created May 25, 1809—became 2nd Voltigeurs
December 30, 1810.

Conscrits-Grenadiers
1st Regiment created March 29, 1809—became 3rd Tirailleurs
February 10, 1811.

2nd Regiment created March 31, 1809—became 4th Tirailleurs February 10, 1811.

Conscrits-Chasseurs

1st Regiment created March 31, 1809—became 3rd Voltigeurs February 10, 1811.

2nd Regiment created March 31, 1809—became 4th Voltigeurs February 10, 1811.

Velites of Turin created April 1809

Velites of Florence created April 1809

(Gardes nationales de la Garde) created January 1, 1810—became 7th Voltigeurs February 15, 1813.

(Sapeurs de Genie) created July 16, 1810—disbanded 1814—reformed April 8, 1815.

Tirailleurs

1st Regiment created from 1 Tirailleur-grenadiers December 30, 1810—reformed April 8, 1815.

2nd Regiment created from 2 Tirailleur-grenadiers December 30, 1810—reformed April 8, 1815.

3rd Regiment created from 1 Conscrit-grenadiers February 10, 1811 reformed April 8, 1815.

3rd bis regiment created from Pupilles January 17, 1813—disbanded March 1813.

4th Regiment created from 4 Conscrit-grenadiers February 10, 1811—reformed April 8, 1815.

4th bis Regiment created from Pupilles January 17, 1813—disbanded March, 1813.

5th Regiment created May 18, 1811—reformed April 8, 1815.

5th bis Regiment created from Pupilles January 17, 1813—disbanded March 1813.

6th Regiment created August 28, 1811—reformed April 8, 1815.

6th bis Regiment created January 10, 1813—disbanded March 1813.

7th Regiment created January 17, 1813—reformed May 12, 1815.

8th Regiment created March 23, 1813—reformed May 12, 1815.

9th-13th Regiments created April 6, 1813—disbanded 1814.

14th-16th Regiments created January 11, 1813—disbanded 1814.

17th-19th Regiments created January 21, 1814—disbanded 1814.

Voltigeurs

1st Regiment created from 1 Tirailleur-chasseurs December 30, 1810—reformed April 8, 1815.

2nd Regiment created from 2 Tirailleur-chasseurs December 30, 1810—reformed April 8, 1815.

3rd Regiment created from 1 Conscrit-chasseurs February 10, 1811, reformed April 8, 1815.

3rd bis Regiment created from Pupilles January 17, 1813—disbanded March, 1813.

4th Regiment created from 2 Conscrit-chasseurs February 10, 1811—reformed April 8, 1815.

4th bis regiment created January 17, 1813—disbanded March 1813.

5th Regiment created May 18, 1811—reformed April 8, 1815.

5th bis Regiment created January 17, 1813—disbanded March, 1813.

6th Regiment created August 28, 1811—reformed April 8, 1815.
6th bis Regiment created January 10, 1813—disbanded March 1813.
7th Regiment created from National Guards of the Guard
February 15, 1813—reformed May 12, 1815.
8th Regiment created March 23, 1813—reformed May 12, 1815.
9th-13th Regiments created April 6, 1813—disbanded 1814.
14th-16th Regiments created January 21, 1814—
disbanded 1814.
17th-19th Regiments created January 21, 1814—
disbanded 1814.
Pupilles created March 30, 1811—disbanded 1814.
Flanqueur-grenadiers created September 4, 1812—
disbanded 1814.
Flanqueur-chasseurs created March 23, 1813—disbanded 1814.

Appendix 4: Band Formations

UNFORTUNATELY there is no completely authenticated source which shows the position of the musicians and composition of the bands of the Imperial Guard. Contemporary prints are not very clear on the matter and the layouts shown below are theoretical.

The legend for the various instruments is as follows:
C. Clarinet, F. Flute, H. Hautbois, B. Bassoon, T. Trumpet, TR. Trombone, HO. French Horn, S. Serpent, BD. Bass Drum (Grosse Caisse), LD. Long Drum (Caisse roulante), D. Side drum, TL. Triangle, CY. Cymbals, CC. Chapeau Chinois, DM Drum major, DS. Drum master, BM. Band master.

Layout of a large band, in this particular case based on the available details on the Chasseurs à pied.

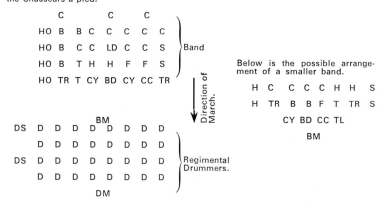

Below is the possible arrangement of a smaller band.

Appendix 5: Alphabetical Glossary of Terms and Orders of Dress

Aiguillettes	A cord shoulder strap with an ornamental knot from which loops of plain and plaited cords hung, fastening to a lapel buttonhole or on to the chest.
Baguette	Drum stick.
Bicorne	A broad brimmed hat with the edges turned up on two opposite sides. Worn fore and aft or sideways.